Keto Meal Prep Cookbook 2018

The Ultimate Guide of Keto Diet Meal Prep for Beginners to Lose Weight, Save Time & Money, and Have Low Carb Dishes

By Dr. Andrea Miller

Contents

Introduction

Are you struggling with overweight and obesity issues? Have you tried everything from fad diet to supplements and have got no results of weight loss? Are you in Keto Diet or want to dive into it? If yes, then you have purchased a book that is going to change your life and perception.

Keto diet is high in fats, moderate in proteins, and low in carbs. People who follow a Keto Diet usually want to lose weight. But it is not only can help people lose excess fat, it also has many other benefits by following it!

This complete **Keto Meal Prep Cookbook** introduces you to the concept of ketosis, how it works, and how to turn yourself into a fat burner. It explains how you can set your macronutrient targets and the ways to monitor your carb intake. It gives detailed information about the benefits of a keto diet and how to be in ketosis.

With the help of this book, you can formulate a diet chart for yourself and prepare yourself to fight keto flu, a common symptom of ketosis that lasts for a few days.

Some effective exercises techniques and do's & don'ts of keto Diet are explicitly detailed in the book. Please go through the FAQ section to clear doubts, if any.

A major part of the book is dedicated to helping you prepare for the keto diet. **This book will guide you about the keto staples and pantry and how to manage things in a keto kitchen.** From preserving veggies to preparing condiments, you will find everything in this book.

The latter part of the book is nothing short of a treat. I have Written plenty of delicious and easy-to-make keto-friendly recipes that you can try, including: *breakfast, lunch, dinner, snacks, soups, salads, desserts and drinks.* I am sure you will like all of them!

So, dear readers let us eat fat to deplete fat. To unveil more secrets of the keto world, please read further.

Part 1- Essentials of Keto diet

Have you ever come across the term "keto diet or ketosis"? If no, don't be worried. You are not alone to be introduced to this amazing concept for the first time. Before we move any further, it is very important to explain to you what a keto diet is all about. So dear readers, let us begin this wonderful journey of this book with a bright hope in our heart that you will not only follow the keto diet but will be able to reap its benefits too.

Chapter 1: Know about Keto Diet and It's Macros

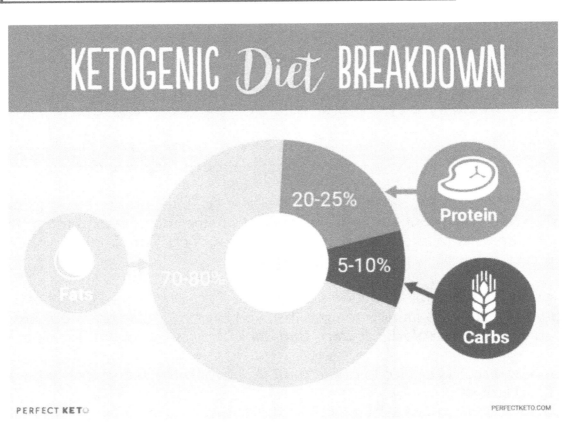

Keto diet was created by Dr. Gianfranco Cappello, an associate professor of surgery at the Sapienza University in Rome, Italy.

A keto diet or Ketogenic diet is primarily a high-fat, moderate-protein, and very low carbohydrate diet that stimulates your body to synthesis "ketones" in the liver that are utilized as energy. The idea is to make your body burn as many fats as it can rather than the carbs.

Though the keto diet is a known way to treat epilepsy, especially in children, it has not one but many benefits. Keto diet is also known as **low-carb high-fat diet (LCHF)**.

Let us know something more about the keto diet.

Do you know that the high-carb diet results in the production of glucose and insulin? So, what happens when glucose and insulin are produced?

Glucose is very easy for your body to be converted to energy and is thus considered over any other energy source and insulin processes the produced glucose. Since your body has ample glucose at its disposal, it doesn't utilize the fats and thus, they are stored in your body.

Now, the idea of keto diet is to limit and starve your body of glucose so that it enters into a state known as "ketosis".

Ketosis is a state that your body naturally adapts to in the situation when there is a deficit of carbohydrates. Your body produces "**ketones**" in the liver that are used to burn fats. Thus, your body finds itself in an active metabolic state which is achieved by starving it of carbohydrates and not calories.

Always remember that the human physiology is extremely adaptive. You starve your body of carbohydrates and replace it with fats, ketosis is bound to happen.

Is keto diet suitable for me?

The keto diet is gaining huge popularity among masses nowadays, but a very important question that arises here is that whether this diet is safe and beneficial. Dr. G. Capello's keto diet has proved to be a magic wand for literally thousands of dieters. They claim to have dropped weight rapidly with few side effects.

Dieters claim to have lost almost 22 pounds by following 2.5 cycles of the diet with manageable side effects.

Keto diet has plenty of benefits that you can look up to.

- ✓ If your motive is to shed weight then there is good news for you. Your body quickly responds to the keto diet and you get some amazing results in very less time. This keeps you encouraged and motivated.
- ✓ It is quite a simple concept as you need to eliminate a particular category of foods and formulate your diet plan on the basis of the acceptable foods.
- ✓ Though you eliminate a major source of energy i.e. carbs, you still feel full and the energy level is also up.
- ✓ Your blood sugar remains in control. Keto diet is the best answer to Type 2 diabetes.
- ✓ It improves the insulin quality and sensitivity of your body.

However, there are a few drawbacks too that you need to know in advance.

- ❖ It is a very strict dieting approach.
- ❖ Small discrepancies in the program will render it useless.
- ❖ It is different for everyone. Thus, the results cannot be generalized. It can be an amazing experience for one, while terrible for the other.
- ❖ You can lose muscle mass and feel fatigued.
- ❖ It is a short-term approach and thus weight-gain can be triggered once the diet is over.

Thus, my advice to you is to consider keto diet if you are trying to shed weight. But always consult your doctor and follow it for a brief period of time. Please don't go to any extreme.

Macronutrient targets

Before taking up the Ketogenic diet, it is important that you know and reach your nutrition targets. Then you will be benefited from the program.
Keto calculator (https://www.ruled.me/keto-calculator) is designed to help you determine your macronutrient intake while you are on a keto diet.
Keto calculator measures the macronutrient target on the basis of:
- Gender
- Age
- Weight in Lbs
- Height in feet and inches
- Activity level whether sedentary, less active, moderately active, very active, or athlete
- Body fat percentage (measured using a skinfold calipers or body measurement method)
- Amount of carbs you want to consume per day. E.g. 2 grams

Your macronutrients

The macronutrient values given below will help you achieve your keto diet goals successfully. Try to follow the values as much as possible, though a small variation won't cause much difference. Also, consider that the energy requirements differ on the basis of the activity level. So nothing is scripted on a stone.
First, let us see the macro requirements on a stable weight.

Stable weight

You need to know your BMR (Basal Metabolic Rate). It can be calculated by Mifflin - St Jeor Formula. For example:

BMR: 1515 kcal

Calories consumption: 2000kcal

Fat intake: 171 grams

Then, the macronutrient requirement is as below:

Net carbs	Proteins	Fats
25 grams	92 grams	171 grams
100 kcal	366kcal	1534kcal
5%	18%	77%

Weight loss goal (12-36%) calorie deficit

- **Small calorie deficit (12%)**
  Calories to be consumed: 1760kcal
  Fat intake should be: 144grams

Net carbs	Proteins	Fats
25 grams	92 grams	144 grams
100 kcal	366kcal	1294kcal
6%	21%	73%

- **Moderate calorie deficit (24%)**
  Calories to be consumed: 1520kcal
  Fat intake should be: 117grams

Net carbs	Proteins	Fats
25 grams	92 grams	117grams
100 kcal	366kcal	1054kcal
7%	24%	69%

- **Large calorie deficit (36%)**
  Calories to be consumed: 1280kcal
  Fat intake should be: 91grams

Net carbs	Proteins	Fats
25 grams	92 grams	91grams
100 kcal	366kcal	814kcal
8%	29%	36%

We generally have the macros distributed in the following range:

> ➢ 60-75% fats
> ➢ 15-30% proteins
> ➢ 5-10% carbs

Mostly the keto diets restrict their carbs to just 5%.

What are the healthy fats?

A fat is nothing less than a blessing only if you select the right type. The problem is that we are so much afraid of the term "fat", that in order to avoid it, we replace it with some bad options like refined carbs and subsequently miss out on plenty of benefits that fats bring along.

Here is how you can select the right kind of fat without making any terrible choices.

1. Polyunsaturated fats

Your goal should be to get as much as you can from the fats. These are extremely important for the development of your brain, neurological system, and overall body development.

Nuts, fish oil, seeds, and vegetable oil are some known examples. These are also known as bad cholesterol reducing agents.

2. Unsaturated fats

These are the undisputed good guys. These are in a liquid state at the room temperature. Olive oil, vegetable oil, unsalted nuts, and seafood are rich sources of unsaturated fats. Unsaturated fats contribute a lot to the development of body, enhancing metabolism, and especially keeping the cardio-vascular system health.

3. Monounsaturated fats

Monounsaturated fats limit bad cholesterol and raise the level of HDL or good cholesterol. Olive oil, peanut oil, seeds, nuts, and avocados are rich sources of monounsaturated fats.

All you need to do is to make a few replacements here and there. Peanut oil for stir fry or hummus instead of sour cream are not only healthy but delicious replacements.

4. Omega-3 fatty acids

These are the super healthy and indispensable fats needed by your body. These superstars help in the brain development, cure inflammation, help in blood coagulation, and maintain blood pressure and triglyceride level. Fish oil, fatty fish, nuts, seeds, and seafood are rich in omega-3 fatty acids.

The healthy fats list given above has "0 net carbs per unit" along with other benefits. These should be an important part of your daily menu, especially while following the keto diet.
Trans-fats, omega-6 fatty acids, and cholesterol are other types of fats. These come in the "not so healthy category". Make sure you either limit their consumption or eliminate if possible.

<u>Amazing Benefits of saturated fats</u>

Saturated fats are the known evil guys. Ironically, they are not as evil as depicted. Rather, your body needs them to a certain limit. Below are a few reasons why are these fats not so bad.

- ✓ A little quantity of saturated fats in the meal decreases cardiovascular risk. A portion of saturated fats in the food helps in reducing the level of lipoprotein that is a known enemy of the cardiovascular health.
- ✓ Saturated fats enhance the absorption of the calcium by bones. Thus, you get stronger bones and healthier bone density.
- ✓ Your liver is saved from the damage caused by medications, painkillers, and high dosage drugs if you incorporate a portion of saturated fats in your diet.
- ✓ Your brain is a mass of fat and cholesterol. Thus, healthy saturated fats are always required for its proper functioning.
- ✓ These also aid in the proper nerve functioning and signaling.
- ✓ Saturated fats boost your immune system as these are important components of the WBC.
- ✓ Saturated fats raise the level of good cholesterol in your blood and thus many heart-related diseases are prevented.
- ✓ In continuation to the last point, the myth that saturated fats risk our heart health stands debunked. There is no relevant and scientific evidence to support this myth.
- ✓ Consumption of a portion of saturated fats is known to reduce the chances of stroke.

- ✓ As saturated fats are not oxidized easily when exposed to heat, they do not form toxic by-products. It is thus advisable to use coconut oil or butter when you have to cook food at a very high temperature.
- ✓ The foods choices are innumerable and nutritious. Eggs, grass-fed beef and cows, butter, and other dairy products are a few examples to quote.
- ✓ Get over the myth that a high-fat diet causes you to gain weight. It is a partial truth. The truth is that such diets do not contain pure fats but added carbs and sugars too. The food thus makes you gain weight and the blame is laid on the fats alone. Contrary to this, a high-saturated fat diet may actually help you in shedding weight.
- ✓ Last but not the least, these taste straight from heaven. What is the value of a life without cheese? Nothing if you ask me.

Please Watch out for fractional carbs!

Here is a word of caution for you. When you buy food products, the manufacturers usually fail to notify what we call the "fractional carbs". Say for example you buy a heavy cream and it has less than 1 gram of carbohydrates per tsp and the label on the pack shows 0 grams.

Now you make a dish and use maybe 2 cups from the same cream. You do not realize, but out of the 20 grams daily carbohydrate allowance, you have already utilized 2 grams.

Thus, it is very important for you to watch out for the fractional carbs.

Here is a small list that might be helpful to you in some way.

- ❖ A rib steak is anyone's favorite food especially while eating out. A 5.5-ounce serving will provide you with 17 grams of fat, 30 grams of protein, and 2.7 grams of carbohydrates. Now you will say what? Does meat have carbs? Yes, my dear. You should make a habit of getting the nutritional information of any food that you consume and then you will get amazed to know about its nutrition distribution.
- ❖ Fractions of carbs in vegetables add up really quick if you do not keep track of the value.
- ❖ A 3.5 ounce of raw asparagus contains less than 2 grams of carbs per serving. It means that if you cook it along with other low-carb options, you will end up consuming too many carbs.
- ❖ A medium-sized cabbage head contains 5.8 grams of carbs. To limit the carb intake, consume 1 medium-sized cabbage head in at least 8 servings.
- ❖ Extract 6 servings for a medium-sized cauliflower head. 3.6 ounces of cauliflower contains 5 grams of carbohydrates.

- ❖ Mushrooms are loved by one and all. 5 whole mushrooms yield around 3.3 grams of carbs.
- ❖ 5 radishes add up to 3.4 grams of carbs to your diet. This is very low and thus a great option for a keto diet.
- ❖ This might amaze you, but one serving of onions contains a whopping 9.3 grams of carbs. Do not eat more than half a serving.
- ❖ 7 broccoli florets contain 6.6 grams of carbs.
- ❖ 1 serving of celery has 3 grams of carbs.
- ❖ I medium-sized zucchini yield 3 grams of carbs.
- ❖ Red, yellow, and green pepper bells have 6, 6.3, and 4.6 grams of carbs per serving respectively.
- ❖ 1 cucumber serving has 3.6 grams of carbs.

By going through these points, I am sure you would be astonished. You have always heard that who turns fat eating veggies? Well, true. But they didn't tell you that too much of the high-carb vegetable won't let you stay in ketosis for long.

The bad influences of over-consuming carbs

Carbs are considered the notorious nutrients because of some health-related issues they bring along. The fault, however, is not of the carbs alone. People consume too many of the carbs in short intervals. Problems are thus bound to occur.

We should also not fail to acknowledge the fact that these are one of the most important and best sources of energy for our body. But as rightly said, "excess of everything is bad".

Let me point out a few known health issues that over-consumption of carbs leads to.

- **Weight gain**
  If consumed in limits, the same carbs promote weight loss by providing energy to your body while you workout. But they turn your enemies if you over-consume them.
  Your body stores the surplus carbs in the form of adipose tissue. So, it is advisable to keep your carb intake in limits and reap the benefits of it without any side-effects.

- **Type 2 diabetes**
  Among several other disorders related to carb overconsumption, Type 2 diabetes is the worst. It happens when your body either stops the synthesis of insulin or produces it in less quantity.

Insulin is the key enzyme to convert the glucose into energy. In the advent of carb-overconsumption, your blood sugar level rises and the insulin production may halt.

- **Unhealthy fats**
  Triglycerides are the evil and unhealthy fats moving in your bloodstream. Well, unfortunately, they are good friends of carbs. You consume carbs in excess and the level of triglycerides is bound to rise.
  Heart-related disorders, swollen arteries, and blood clots in vital organs are a few problems caused by high triglyceride levels.

- **Swollen arteries**
  Food rich in carbohydrates is often rich in fats too. Irrespective of the fact whether the fat is healthy or unhealthy, it has a potential to form a thin layer in your arteries, causing it to thicken.
  The passage of blood through thick arteries restricts it flow and you become vulnerable to heart-attacks and strokes. In order to keep this atherosclerosis beast in the cage, consume carbs in limits.

- **Brain fog**
  Cognitive functioning of an individual gets hampered if too many carbs are consumed. Ask a diabetic who has experienced the terrible frustration, agitation, irritability, nervousness, and confusion caused due to brain fog. All of these are not at all funny.

You should remember that too many carbs mean too many problems. Portion your carb intake and see the benefits coming your way.

Calculate your own proper carb intake

When you are following the keto diet, you need to find the optimum carb level suited to your needs. You can either take the total carbs or net carbs into consideration.
Net carbs= Total carbs – Fiber
When you are in Ketosis, you should consume 50 grams or less of total carbs, which means less than 30 grams of net carbs.

How Many Carbs Intake per Day to Stay in Ketosis?

Ketosis won't be achieved unless you highly restrict your daily carb intake. In general, 20-100 grams of carbohydrate consumption per day leads you to the state of ketosis. Though 100 grams is very rare, for most of the people, 20-30 grams has worked wonders.
There are two methods to identify your ideal carb intake:

1. Low to High method

Start with a very low daily carb intake, suppose 20 grams. When you find yourself in a state of ketosis in coming 3 days, subsequently increase 5 grams per week. You will soon start realizing the state of very less or no ketosis.

On the basis of that, you can conveniently discover your net carb limit. Though it sounds difficult to completely give up the most delicious and known energy source, but give this method a try. It is really worth it.

2. High to Low method

This is the opposite of the above-mentioned method. You start with a high-carb intake like 50 grams and then keep reducing 5 grams per week till you find yourself in a state of ketosis. Though the method sounds less difficult, it is not the recommended one.

Be patient if you can't detect ketones. It will take a couple of days. You are bound to shed kilos when you go keto.

Please note that you don't need to go carb-free. 20-30 grams is an optimal carb intake level and consuming below that won't help you anyway.

The proper protein consumption

Your protein consumption largely depends on your lean mass and how active your lifestyle is.
Lean mass = Total body weight – Fat

It is a bit tricky to identify optimal protein consumption because too many can stop ketosis and too less can cause muscle loss.

Let us see how to find out the optimal protein intake.

Ideal protein intake = Lean mass * Activity level determining factor

The multiplying factor is taken to be between 0.6 to 1 grams/pound or 1.3 to 2.2 grams/kg of the lean mass.

Suppose you weigh 160 pounds and your body-fat is 30%, then your lean mass is calculated as:

160Lbs *(1– 30%) = 112 Lbs

Thus, your protein intake:

112 * 0.6 = 67 grams

112 * 1.0 = 112 grams

67 grams is the minimum and 112 grams is the maximum protein requirement of your body.

This is how you calculate protein intake on the basis of your activity level:

- **For a sedentary lifestyle:** 0.6 * lean weight in Lbs
- **For light activity:** 0.7 * Lean body weight in Lbs
- **For moderate activity:** 0.8 * Lean body weight in Lbs
- **For very active lifestyle:** 0.9 * Lean body weight in Lbs
- **For athletic activity:** 1 * Lean body weight in Lbs

Chapter 2: A Deeper Look Inside Keto Diet

The benefits of being Keto-adapted

First of all, let me make you familiar with the term "**keto-adaptation**". It is the time your body takes to adapt to burn fats instead of carbs.

Turning a fat-burner from a carb-burner is a large-scale metabolic change. Your body needs time, less for some and more for others.

A study found that it takes 3 weeks for the glycogen tanks to deplete, and then the process of ketosis gains momentum. Your body slowly and progressively adapts to burn fats for fuel.

Now, let us discuss a few benefits of being keto-adapted

- You maintain a healthy weight.
- By lowering insulin level in the body, the body is relieved of oxidative stress. This, in turn, slows down aging.
- Keto-adapted individuals run a less or literally negligible risk of having Type 2 diabetes.
- The cardiovascular health of keto-adaptive people is great. They are less vulnerable to heart attacks and strokes.
- PCOS (Polycystic Ovary Syndrome) usually occurs with insulin resistance. A keto-adapted lady has an optimal body weight, insulin level, and other hormonal parameters. Thus, PCOS is avoided.
- Keto-adaptation helps in improving the functioning of the brain. Studies show a 25% increase in the brain efficiency with ketones as the fuel rather than glucose.
- Keto-adapted people are less prone to IBS (Irritable Bowel Syndrome).
- Keto-adapted people have athletic endurance and performance.
- Lower inflammation, healthy gut, stable energy levels, and healthy liver are some common traits of being keto-adapted.

The unwanted symptoms during a keto diet

Ketosis is an amazing way to reduce weight and regain good health; however, it comes with its own set of drawbacks. There are some come temporary side effects of ketosis. This is known as "keto flu", "low carb flu", or "induction flu".

What is keto flu?

When you at once start avoiding the carbohydrate-rich diet, your body considers it as a problem and starts retaliating. You may experience nausea, irritation, laziness, and fatigue. This is known as keto flu.

The symptoms start appearing usually from 3rd to 5th day and may last for a couple of days. For a few, it might take even 10 or more days for the symptoms to fade away.

The Symptoms of Keto Flu

The symptoms of common flu and keto flu are almost the same. Let us take a look at a few.

➢ Anxiety, fatigue, and weakness
➢ Headaches
➢ Dizziness
➢ Irresistible craving for sugar
➢ Mood swings
➢ Diarrhea
➢ Brain fog
➢ Blurry focus
➢ Nausea and vomiting
➢ Sleeplessness
➢ Stomach pain and cramps
➢ Sore muscles

Other symptoms may include thirst, loss of appetite, dry mouth, and bad-breath or keto-breath.

Don't worry; these symptoms will go away in no time. These are just a way in which your body is communicating to you that there is an undesirable change. It will soon adapt to the change and everything will normalize.

How to keep the ketosis at an optimum level

Let us first discuss what optimum ketone range is. Later we shall discuss the ways to maintain it.

Optimal Ketone Range

When the ketones in your blood are in a range of 0.5mM/dL, your body enters the state of ketosis. The optimal range of ketones in the blood to promote weight loss is 1.5-3.0mM/dL.

This is a perfect range wherein you can extract long-term health benefits and lose weight simultaneously.

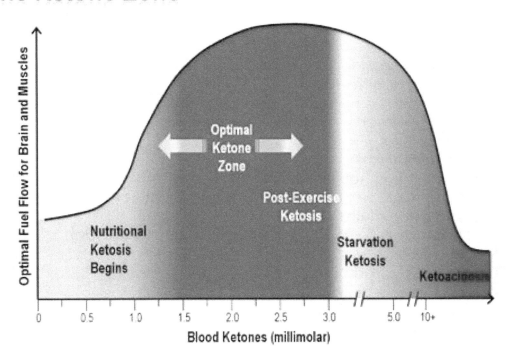

From the graph provided above, you can make out that the green zone depicts the perfect ketone level. Starvation ketosis and beyond are not only dangerous but useless too.

Now, let us discuss a few methods by which you can maintain an optimal ketone level in your blood.

> **Consume less carbs**
> I have discussed since the start of this book that ketosis cannot be achieved unless you minimize your carb intake. Less carb intake promotes the body to utilize fats instead of glucose and thus, fat is used as an energy source.

You have to watch your net carb and total carb intake to get an idea of how much carbs you are allowed to consume per day.

> **Don't eliminate the carbs completely**
We usually observe that instead of restricting the carb intake, many people go carb-less. This not only has a bad effect on their health, it also disrupts the process of ketosis. To maintain an optimal ketone level, you should consume at least 20-30grams of carbs per day.

> **Coconut oil**
Consuming coconut oil helps you to maintain ketone level. As coconut oil contains MCT (Medium-chain triglycerides), these are conveniently absorbed by your liver and at once converted into ketones.

> **Exercise and workout**
Exercise and workout help your body to be in ketosis. It has been observed that dieters who are active and exercise regularly are able to deplete more of their glycogen tanks, produce more ketones, and thus get into ketosis easily.

> **Consume more healthy fats**
Healthy fats boost the production of ketones. A typical keto diet contains 60-80% of fats. The catch is to choose the right kind of fat like olive oil, avocados, butter, and tallow.

> **Go for intermittent fast**
Don't eat for a few hours once or twice a week. It is a great way to get into ketosis. It also helps to maintain an optimal ketone level and improves results.

> **Have adequate proteins**
Have moderate proteins that suffice your needs but don't consume them excessively. Protein supply amino acids to the liver which helps in producing glucose for a few organs that can't use ketones. Proteins also help in maintaining muscle density while you shed weight.

> **Test your ketone levels and make necessary adjustments**
You can test the presence of ketones through a blood, breath, or urine test. You come to know whether you are in the optimal range or not, and then make necessary adjustments in your diet if required.

Tips for a Keto journey

Ketosis is not very easy to practice. However, with some quick tips, you can definitely increase your chances of making your keto journey a success.
Let me put forth some quick tips for a great ketosis.

✓ **Intermittent fasting**: fasting for a few hours naturally makes your body to deplete the excess glucose. Thus, the body starts consuming fats and ketosis occurs.

- ✓ **Decrease anxiety and stress**: ketosis fails when you are under a lot of stress. If you have any stress, it is better to undertake a stress management program or follow a relaxation technique before you start your keto diet.
- ✓ **Sleep**: get at least 7-9 hours of sleep daily.
- ✓ **Increase sodium intake**: add an extra dash of salt in your diet. It will help you with ketosis.
- ✓ **Exercise**: the more you workout, the more glucose will be consumed.
- ✓ **Have moderate proteins**: excess proteins are no less harmful to ketosis as carbs. So have protein in moderate amounts and not more.
- ✓ Drink as much water as you can.
- ✓ Consume carbs from veggies instead of starch or refined carbs.
- ✓ Use Medium-chain triglyceride oils like coconut oil. They help in sustaining the body in ketosis.
- ✓ Try to have a healthy gut to improve insulin sensitivity.
- ✓ Always measure food on a scale. An extra tbsp sometimes means more 5 grams of carbs and 100 more calories.
- ✓ Take a good quality ketone supplement.
- ✓ Count every carb you take.
- ✓ Use a keto stick to see if you are in a state of ketosis.

By following these simple tips, I am sure you will emerge successfully for your keto diet journey and you will fall in love with the slim and healthier version of yourself.

Common mistakes to be avoided

By avoiding some common mistakes in a keto diet, you can double your chances of losing weight and becoming a fat-burner. The idea is to eat right and follow right.

Let us point out some common keto diet mistakes

- ❖ **Being unaware of your macros**
  As you know, a Ketogenic diet means low cars, moderate proteins, and high fats. So, by consuming less carbs and not monitoring your protein and fat intake, you are moving away from your target. Keep a track of all the three macros.
- ❖ **Having carb-phobia**
  Many of you think the just by eating less carbs or going carb-free, you will enter ketosis and shed weight. Sorry to say, but this isn't true. You need to understand that your body should get some daily net carbs. This will not only aid the formation of ketones, it will, in fact, assist you a lot with weight loss.
- ❖ **Protein-inadequacy**

Eat sufficient protein. It has a great role to play in the ketosis. I am not asking you to go beyond the recommended levels, but don't consume under that either. It provides fuel to some major organs of the body like kidneys by forming glucose in the absence of carbs.

❖ **Not getting enough fats**
Fat is responsible for providing fuel to your body when it is in a state of ketosis. A major portion of your diet should consist of healthy fats like omega-3 fatty acids. The catch is to choose the right kind of fat. Then only the purpose of ketosis will be fulfilled.

❖ **Not consuming veggies and fiber**
Always consume plenty of veggies, greens, and fiber. These are high in nutrition and less in carbs. This will positively impact your ketosis.

❖ **The ketone-craze**
Daily and hourly monitoring of ketones won't benefit you in any way. The optimal range is between 0.5-3.0mM/dL. Going into starvation ketosis or more will result in nothing good. Don't fall prey to the question that if I have a high ketone reading, why am I not losing weight?

❖ **The stress monster**
Stress yields nothing fruitful but takes a lot. It not only takes a toll on your health, it renders your whole ketosis process worthless. Before taking up the keto diet, I strongly advise you to go for stress management classes, breathing, and relaxation techniques.

❖ **Sleep deprivation**
Less sleep means more weight. People who are sleep deprived have a weak glucose metabolism and thus store more fats. You should try to get 7-9 sleep hours daily. Have a light dinner, switch off the electronic gadgets, and have proper ambiance for quick sleep onset.

❖ **Overeating nuts**
Nuts are rich in calories and easy to munch. You don't realize that you have consumed over 700 kcal by consuming just 100 grams of nuts. Have nuts in limit and you will see how beneficial they are. Just don't overeat.

❖ **Having excessive dairy**
In order to fulfill your fat needs of a keto diet, there is a high probability that you consume a lot of fat-full dairy. Coconut oil, avocados, butter, and cream are a few great healthy fat options. Then why to go for dairy alone? Dairy contains a type of protein that can cause insulin spikes. So better have it in limits.

❖ **Consuming a lot of low-carb food**
You may falsely believe that low-carb foods won't hamper your ketosis. That is wrong. Low-carb treats are bad for ketosis and in fact, may increase your carb cravings. Better to avoid them as much as you can. Grab a piece of dark chocolate instead.

- ❖ **Getting fooled by the low-carb label**
  We all know that foods labeled as low carb are actually not. So why to go for such foods? So, it is better to eat real food than the processed pseudo-low-carb food.
- ❖ **Not exercising**
  Many of us believe that by just following the keto diet, things will work out. Well, you should know that exercising helps a lot in the production of ketones. Exercise the right way and you will see the results coming your way pretty soon.

Apart from these, drinking a lot of coffee, alcohol, snacking a lot, having unplanned meals, relying completely on the generic diet, having cheat treats, drinking less water, and poor health conditions also are very common problems that can make the keto diet futile.

Do's and Don'ts of Keto diet

The benefits of going keto are manifold. You shed weight, get rid of diabetes, hypertension, and other health disorders. If you follow some do's and don'ts, believe me, the success is guaranteed.
Let us have a quick look at a few do's and don'ts of a keto diet.

Do's of a keto diet
- Eat a lot of low-starch veggies, grass-fed beef, chicken, salmon, heavy cream, and butter.
- Have a lot of electrolytes. Have bone broth, chicken stock, and vegetable broth. Add more salt to your food.
- Consume ample healthy fats. It is the food for your brain. Coconut oil, avocados, olive oil, butter, heavy cream, butter, MCT oil, and nuts are a few options.
- Use natural sweeteners like Stevia and not the chemical ones like Splenda.
- Do monitor your protein and fat intake.
- Count your carbs.
- Avoid processed food. It is bad for the ketosis.

Don'ts of a keto diet
- Don't eat what we call "sugar-free" jellies, candies, low-carb processed food, sugar-free chocolates, shakes, or diet soda. It not only contains plenty of sugar, it will disrupt your whole ketosis process.
- Don't eat food low in fat. Rather, eat a lot of high-fat cheese, yogurt, and other foods. You need a lot of fat while you are on a keto diet.

- Don't be obsessed with a keto scale. When you are in ketosis, fat is bound to burn and weight is bound to shed. So chill.

Chapter 3: Formulating a Keto Diet for Weight Loss and Healing

It is absolutely necessary that you formulate a proper keto diet chart that you will follow. There should be specific recipes for breakfast, lunch, dinner, snack, and desserts that will induce ketosis.

In the latter part of the book, I will present some quick recipes for the different meals of the day. For now, let me formulate a small 3-day keto diet plan for your convenience and as an idea how to go about the keto diet.

Have a look at the table below.

Day	Breakfast	Lunch	Dinner	Snacks	Dessert	Nutritional value
1	Crust-less Bacon with cheddar cheese	BLT chicken salad	Beef stew or pork chops	½ avocado with a dash of salt	1 piece of dark chocolate	1589 calories, 14g carbs, 85g protein, 134g fat
2	Cheese-egg omelet and tea	2 cups baby spinach with 2 roasted chicken thighs	Crust-less Bacon with cheddar cheese and a plate of green salad	2 strings of cheese with bacon	1 piece of dark chocolate	1449 calories, 17g carbs, 72g protein, 126g fat
3	Cream cheese pancakes	Beef fast salad	Grilled Salmon with green beans and butter	6 salted almonds	1 piece of dark chocolate	1485 calories, 19gcarbs, 68g protein, 127g fat.

Following this sample table, you can make a 3 or 4-week keto diet chart for yourself. The recipes that will be discussed later will be of much help to you.

Using Exercise Effectively in a Keto Life

You should exercise a lot when you are on a keto diet. There are plenty of health benefits and you will feel energy boosted all the time. The myth that a low-carb diet and exercise do not go hand in hand is long gone.

Let us discuss how to exercise effectively in ketosis. The conventional idea of eating less and doing workout and exercise for long hours is outdated. Keto is the new trend. Eating healthy and doing effective exercise is making rounds nowadays.

Keto workout is typically classified in the following 4 categories.

4 TYPES OF EXERCISE IN KETOSIS

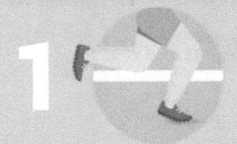

AEROBIC EXERCISE
Ex. Cardio
Long Duration - Low Intensity
Fat Burning

ANAEROBIC EXERCISE
Ex. Weight Lifting or HIIT
Short Duration - High Intensity
Carb Burning

FLEXIBILITY EXERCISES
Ex. Yoga, Stretching
Support Soft-Tissue
Increased Range of Motion

STABILITY EXERCISES
Ex. Balance and Core Training
Supports Alignment,
Improves Balance, Body Control

PERFECT **KET**O

- ➤ **Aerobic exercise:** Cardio exercises that take more than 3 minutes to perform come in this category. Low or steady-state cardio helps a lot in burning fat and is very much recommended to the keto dieters.
- ➤ **Anaerobic exercise:** Weight-training at medium or high-intensity results in short energy bursts. It results in carbohydrate and fat combustion and is a great exercise tip for the keto people. It also helps in keeping the muscles firm.
- ➤ **Flexibility exercises:** Stretching of muscles, joints, and improving muscle motion are all flexibility exercises. These exercises help in keeping the muscles firm and injury-free. Keto dieters should definitely go for these exercises.
- ➤ **Stability exercises:** Balancing and alignment exercises are a part of this group. These exercises are recommended to a keto dieter as they improve the alignment, muscle firmness, and control.

The workout intensity also matters for a keto dieter:

Low-intensity aerobic exercise= combustion of fat as fuel.
High-intensity aerobic exercise= combustion of carbohydrates as fuel.
During ketosis, fat-burning is a must. Thus, anaerobic exercises may seem difficult in the initial phase of the diet but that problem can be solved by using a targeted keto diet for exercise.
It means high-intensity workouts should be backed up by a tailored carb e.g. 30 grams of quick carbs like fruits just before or after a workout. The consumed carbs will help in the workout alone and will not disrupt the ketosis process.

Exercise Tips for Burning More Fat

Here are a few great exercising tips that will help you drop a few pounds while you are on a keto diet. Please take a quick look.

- ✓ First and foremost, your goal should not be to lose fat and burn calories, it should be to feel great and more confident about yourself. Target for long-term and carry out exercises that give tone and strength to your muscles. Fat will drop automatically.
- ✓ Go for moderate intensity cardio exercises like skipping, walking, swimming, or cycling. These help you to burn a lot of calories and you are able to deplete your fat stores.
- ✓ Resistant training is one of the best exercising methods for long-term weight loss. Your focus should primarily be on the major muscles when you go for weight training. Go for squats. This will help you burn fats and form firm muscles.
- ✓ High-intensity intermittent training (HIIT) is the key to promoting the combustion of fats as fuel. In this technique, you take up high-intensity anaerobic exercises

followed by short resting intervals. This is a great way to burn fats in a lesser period of time.

✓ Try lifting weights with 5 reps in a set. Pick a weight that you find heavy.
✓ Skipping or swimming for more than 15 seconds in a set in good for burning fat. 100 meters sprint or 50 meters of freestyle swimming is very beneficial.
✓ Don't overexert yourself. Have a rest day every week and sleep well. Over-doing the exercises promotes the production of stress hormones that hamper your entire process of ketosis.

Chapter 4: Some Frequently Asked Questions about Keto Diet

Here are a few FAQs that I have addressed in this section. Clear your doubts by going through this section quickly.

Q: What is the difference between a low-carb diet and a Ketogenic diet?
A: Any diet that contains less than 130-150 grams of carbs is considered a low-carb diet. However, ketosis is achieved when you consume less than 50 grams, (preferably between 20-30grams) of carb in a day.

Q: Should I keep a count of calories?
A: Ketogenic diet naturally suppresses hunger and you have a tendency to eat less. So, you don't really need to keep a track of the calories.

Q: How should I track my macros?
A: KetoDiet App is a great way to keep a track of your macros.

Q: How often should I eat?
A: Eat when you start to feel hungry. Don't wait for the hunger to grow ravenous. That way you will eat in limit and the cravings will be less.

Q: How much weight will I lose and in how much time?
A: You will most likely lose 1 to 5 Lbs of weight per week.

Q: What is fat fasting?
A: when you fat-fast, 90% of your diet consists of fat while you still manage to keep the calories low between 1000-1200kcal per day. You should practice it for a few days only and it helps you to be in ketosis.

Q: What about fermented foods?
A: Fermented foods like sauerkraut, kombucha, and kimchi are full of nutrition and probiotics. Include these in your keto diet.

Q: Why are many physicians against the keto diet?
A: There can be many reasons. Some physicians follow the old school of thought and some lack information on the keto diet. Also, when a new idea that opposes the general belief emerges, it is usually not accepted.

Q: Will ketosis damage my health?
A: No, you will rather be benefited. Please know the difference between ketosis and ketoacidosis. Ketoacidosis is a health-disorder in which your liver produced 3-5times more ketones than in the normal ketosis. Ketosis, on the other hand, is not only safe but good for your health too.

Q: Should I take any supplements while I am on a keto diet?
A: Take some vitamin, zinc, magnesium, and selenium supplements if possible. It will help you with your keto diet.

Q: Is keto diet safe for pregnant and breastfeeding mothers?
A: Yes it is safe. But, I recommend that the pregnant women and breastfeeding moms should not try to lose weight in the first place.

Q: Can vegetarians and vegans be on a keto diet?

A: Vegetarians can easily follow the keto diet but for vegans, it is really hard to be in ketosis. A vegan diet that is so rich in fats and proteins is comparatively difficult to get and follow.

Q: Can I eat out?

A: Yes, why not. Select meat and beef over starchy foods. A steak with lots of veggies is a great idea to eat out.

Q: How to satisfy my sweet tooth while I am in ketosis?

A: A square of dark chocolate (70% cocoa), Stevia, monk fruit powder, and erythritol are a few "zero-carb" sweeteners. Till you adjust to the new lifestyle, you can go for these.

Q: How to get rid of keto flu?

A: Stay hydrated, have enough electrolytes, relax, and take proper sleep. The symptoms will soon fade away.

I hope I am able to clear most of your doubts. You can anytime hit the internet and find answers to any further quires if any. By now, you must be fully acquainted with the concept and working of ketosis. In the coming chapter, we shall discuss how to go about the process.

Chapter 5- Easy Keto Meal Prep Approach

Dear readers, this chapter is all about shopping, preparations, and creating some mess in the kitchen. It entirely focuses on the preparations you need to make before starting the keto diet.
 So, roll up your sleeves and grab your shopping bags, because we have to buy a lot of delicious foods and we have to spend some gala time in the kitchen.

1. Prepare Your Keto Staples In Advance

A successful meal preparation can be achieved when everything is in the right place and you don't have to hustle around your kitchen trying to grab the right thing. In this section, I will put forth a list of keto staples you need to buy before you start the keto diet.
These should be handy in your kitchen as you require them in most of your keto meals.

Simple keto staples

Just go through the list provided below and if you don't like any of these, then please don't buy. We are here to lose weight, not waste food. Replace that particular item with a substitute of your choice.
Below is a diagram illustrating your keto staples.

BASICS TO STOCK YOUR KITCHEN

KETO PANTRY STAPLES

NUTS & SEEDS

NUT BUTTERS

MCT OIL POWDER

DIJON OR YELLOW MUSTARD

COCONUT FLOUR

ALMOND FLOUR

BAKING SODA & BAKING POWDER

VANILLA EXTRACT

AVOCADO OIL

COCONUT OIL

RED WINE VINEGAR

KETO SWEETENERS

COCOA POWDER

SUGAR-FREE SPICES LIKE:

SALT & PEPPER

THYME

OREGANO

PARSLEY

GARLIC

CELERY SALT

RED PEPPER FLAKES

CINNAMON

PUMPKIN PIE SPICE

FRIDGE OR FREEZER STAPLES

BUTTER

EGGS

CHEESES OF YOUR CHOICE

GROUND BEEF

SOUR CREAM OR PLAIN, UNSWEETENED YOGURT

HEAVY CREAM OR FULL-FAT COCONUT MILK

CREAM CHEESE

HOT SAUCE

MAYONNAISE

COCONUT AMINOS

PERFECT KETO

Keto Pantry Staples

- Nuts and seeds
- Nut butter
- MCT oil powder
- Sugar-free spices like salt and pepper, thyme, oregano, parsley, garlic powder or cloves, celery salt, red pepper flakes, cinnamon, and pumpkin pie spice
- Dijon or yellow mustard
- Coconut flour
- Almond flour
- Baking soda
- Baking powder
- Vanilla extract
- Avocado oil
- Coconut oil
- Red wine vinegar
- Natural keto sweeteners like Swerve, Stevia, erythritol, or monk fruit
- Cocoa powder

Fridge or Freezer Staples

- Butter (grass-fed)
- Eggs (pastured)
- Cheeses
- Ground beef (grass-fed)
- Sour cream
- Unsweetened yogurt
- Heavy cream
- Full-fat coconut milk
- Cream cheese
- Hot sauce
- Mayonnaise
- Coconut aminos

  Once, you have purchased all these food items, you are not ready for the next step. If you have everything well planned in advance, the future course of action will seem easy. After all, well begun is half done.

2. Chop and Refrigerate Vegetables

Veggies are always the best. There is no second thought on this. For a keto diet, however, I recommend veggies that are high in nutrient and low in carbs. As you rightly guessed, greens are an amazing choice to make.

If you are not very fond of greens, then consider the veggies that grow above the ground.

I have provided a detailed list of veggies in a tabular form that you can buy. Please have a look.

Vegetable Name	Serving Size	Total Carbs (g)	Fiber (g)	Net Carbs (g)
Broccoli Raab	100g	2.85	2.7	0.15
Watercress	100g	1.29	0.5	0.79
Nopales	100g	3.33	2.2	1.13
Bok Choi	100g	2.18	1	1.18
Celery	100g	2.97	1.6	1.37
Spinach	100g	3.63	2.2	1.43
Mustard Greens	100g	4.67	3.2	1.47
Asparagus	100g	3.88	2.1	1.78
Radish	100g	3.4	1.6	1.8
Avocado	100g	8.64	6.8	1.84
Arugula	100g	3.65	1.6	2.05
Zucchini	100g	3.11	1	2.11
Swiss Chard	100g	3.74	1.6	2.14
Mushrooms	100g	3.26	1	2.26
Kohlrabi	100g	6.2	3.6	2.6
Tomato	100g	3.89	1.2	2.69
Olives	100g	6	3.2	2.8
Eggplant	100g	5.88	3	2.88
Bell Pepper	100g	4.6	1.7	2.9
Cauliflower	100g	4.97	2	2.97
Cabbage (Green)	100g	6.1	3.1	3
Bamboo Shoots	100g	5.2	2.2	3
Cabbage (White)	100g	5.37	2.3	3.07
Cucumber	100g	3.63	0.5	3.13
Jalapeno Pepper	100g	6.5	2.8	3.7
Artichoke Hearts	100g	5.38	1.5	3.88
Broccoli	100g	6.64	2.6	4.04
Bean Sprouts	100g	5.94	1.8	4.14

Fennel	100g	7.3	3.1	4.2
Okra	100g	7.45	3.2	4.25
Green Beans	100g	6.97	2.7	4.27
Turnips	100g	6.43	1.8	4.63
Snow Peas	100g	7.55	2.6	4.95
Brussels Sprouts	100g	8.95	3.8	5.15
Kale	100g	8.75	3.6	5.15
Cabbage (Red)	100g	7.37	2.1	5.27
Pumpkin	100g	7	1	6
Rutabaga	100g	8.62	2.3	6.32
Carrots	100g	9.58	2.8	6.78
Celeriac	100g	9.2	1.8	7.4
Onion	100g	9.34	1.7	7.64
Leek	100g	14.15	1.8	12.35
Ginger	100g	17.77	2	15.77

From the table, you can make out that every vegetable has a proportion of carbohydrate present in it. So, you need to choose your vegetables and serving size wisely.

Once, you have purchased the desired veggies from the above list, it is time to neatly chop and arrange them in the refrigerator. Below is a step by step guide for you.

➢ Wash the vegetables (except green leafy) thoroughly.
➢ If the vegetable is of the sort that requires peeling like carrots, cucumber, or onion, then peel it.
➢ Chop the vegetables using a chef's knife.
➢ Arrange in separate plastic wraps or foil either on the basis of serving size like 100grams or place each vegetable separately.
➢ Set in the refrigerator.

The table provided below will give you an idea of how to refrigerate different veggies. Most of these should be parboiled before refrigerating. We will talk about it in the coming section.

Artichokes	Sprinkle with a little water and store in a plastic bag.
Asparagus	Wrap stalk ends in damp paper towel and place in a plastic bag.
Beets	Cut off the green tops and refrigerate them separately.
Bell Peppers	Chop and store in a net bag.
Broccoli	Cut the head into florets and store in an open plastic bag in the crisper.
Brussels Sprouts	Keep in a plastic bag.

Cabbage	Chop and store in a net bag in the crisper.
Carrots	Remove the green tops; chop and keep in a net bag in the crisper.
Cauliflower	Cut into florets and store in a net bag in the crisper.
Celery	Chop and store in a plastic bag in the crisper.
Corn	Keep the husks on until ready to cook.
Cucumber	Chop and store in a plastic box.
Eggplant	Keep in a plastic bag.
Green Beans	Chop and store in an airtight container.
Green Onions	Store in a plastic bag.
Kale	Chop and keep in a plastic bag in the crisper.
Leeks	Chop and store in a loosely closed plastic bag.
Lettuce	Keep in a loosely closed plastic bag in the crisper.
Mushrooms	Chop and store in a paper bag.
Peas	Peel and store in a perforated plastic bag.
Radish	Remove the green tops, chop, and store in a net bag.
Spinach	Chop and store in a perforated plastic bag in the crisper.
Turnips	Chop and keep in a plastic box.
Zucchini	Store in a plastic bag.

The vegetables remain fresh and last long in the fridge. You can conveniently use them as a salad or an ingredient when you cook meals.

3. Parboil and Freeze Vegetables

Parboiling or blanching process involves boiling or steaming veggies for a little time so that they turn a bit tender and are semi-cooked. This is a highly recommended step before freezing many veggies like broccoli, greens, beans, okra, etc especially when you are going to prepare a keto meal.

The biggest advantage of parboiling veggies is that it preserves the color, texture, and taste which would otherwise be dull. I am sure you must have seen how dark and messy the spinach turns in just a day if you just dump it in the fridge. When you parboil vegetables, their enzymatic activity disrupts and thus, they don't decay or change color. Some enzymes can thrive and continue the decaying process even in the freezer and such veggies are spoilt even if you keep them in the fridge. By parboiling you literally kill the enzymes.

How to parboil vegetables

- ➢ Boil water in a big pot and in the meantime, rinse, clean, and chop the veggies.
- ➢ Put the veggies into the boiling water or in a steam tray over the boiling water.
- ➢ Boil for the appropriate time suitable for the vegetable. (I will discuss that shortly).
- ➢ Once done, immediately dump the veggies into cold water or put them under a stream of cold water.
- ➢ Drain and squeeze away the water. Make sure very little or no water is left before you freeze the veggies.
- ➢ Put the parboiled veggies in a freezer bag, tray, or container.
- ➢ Make sure you remove air and leave enough headspace.
- ➢ Set in the freezer.

There are few veggies like tomatoes, onion, corn, and peppers that do fine without blenching, while there are others like potatoes that spoil even after parboiling.

Parboiling time for different veggies

This list will guide you on how much time you need to parboil veggies before freezing them.

- Artichoke hearts - 6 minutes
- Asparagus - 2 to 4 minutes (depending on the stalk thickness)
- Beans - 3 minutes
- Broccoli florets - 2 minutes
- Brussels sprouts - 3 to 5 minutes (depending on size)
- Cauliflower florets - 3 minutes
- Kohlrabi cubes - 1 minute
- Leafy greens - 1 to 2 minutes (use the longer time for collards and cabbage)
- Okra - 2 to 3 minutes (depending on size)
- Peas in the pod - 2 to 3 minutes (depending on size)
- Peas shelled - 1.5 minutes
- Squash, Chayote - 2 minutes
- Squash, summer - 3 minutes

You should label the veggies with the date on which you freeze them as even the parboiled veggies can lose nutritional value over a period of time. Frozen vegetables last for 8-10 months and it is advisable to use them in the "best before" period.

4. Freeze Berries and Herbs

Freezing berries

Berries are very delicate and should be carefully handled. Wash them only when you want to use them or they will turn dull and mushy.

This is how you should go about the process of freezing berries:

- ➤ Rinse strawberries under a stream of cold water without removing stems. Dip raspberries, blueberries, and boysenberries in cold water and then drain the water.
- ➤ Spread the berries on a baking sheet in a single layer and pat dry with a paper napkin.
- ➤ Freeze the berries for a couple of days on the tray till they turn solid.
- ➤ Put the frozen berries in separate freezer bags or air-tight containers. Leave some space in the bag as the berries are expected to expand a little.
- ➤ Label each bag with the type of berry, date of freezing, and the quantity.
- ➤ Place the bags in the freezer. Make sure they are flat.
- ➤ Add the packs in small batches and keep some room for the air.
- ➤ Stack the berry bags once deep frozen.
- ➤ Utilize strawberries in 5 days and other berries last up to 12 months.

Freezing herbs

What can be better than using the fresh herbs directly from the kitchen garden? Sadly, herbs do not last long and their shelf life is very low. The most common way to preserve herbs is by drying. However, the aroma doesn't last long nor do the flavors.

Another great way to preserve the herbs is to freeze them. It is an easy process that helps in retaining the flavor, aroma, and nutrients of the herbs. I know they are not pleasant to see and not a good choice for a salad, but the aroma and taste are retained.

The following 4 methods work great for freezing fresh herbs:

➤ **Freezing bare herbs**: Some herbs like thyme, rosemary, dill, bay, and sage can be simply frozen and put in an air-tight container. You have to spread these in a single layer on a tray or plate and set in the freezer. Transfer the frozen herbs to an air-tight container and place the container in the fridge or freezer. Some herbs like chives can be chopped and frozen in a similar fashion with very less flavor loss.

➤ **Freezing in water:** Delicate herbs like mint, parsley, and cilantro can be frozen as ice cubes. Remove the leaves from the stem, chop, wash, and place in the ice tray. Pour water into the tray and place in the freezer. You can later transfer the herb cubes into air-tight containers or bags and place in the freezer.

➤ **Freezing in oil**: Herbs such as basil, thyme, or oregano that are used in soups can be well preserved in oil. Combine the fresh herbs with ¼ cup olive oil and make a thick blend in a food processor. Transfer the blend into ice trays and freeze. You can store the cubes in air-tight containers. If you want to preserve leaves instead of paste, put the leaves in the ice tray, pour oil over them, and freeze.

➤ **Rolled herbs**: Herbs like parsley and sage are preserved by compressing them at the bottom of a sealed Ziploc bag. The bag is rolled around the bunched herbs, sealed with a rubber band, and placed in the freezer.

The frozen berries and herbs make important ingredients when you prepare keto meals. Make sure you freeze them in abundance.

5. Measure Dry Ingredients Ahead

It is very important for you to measure the ingredients you are using. Keto diet consists of 80% fats, 15% proteins, and 5% carbs. Not more than 20-30grams carbs are allowed per day. Similarly, you should be sure about your fat and protein intake. Thus, measuring ingredients is necessary.

I have provided a list of the keto staples in the first part of this chapter, and you can see there are a plenty of dry ingredients that you will use while preparing keto meals. Here are a few methods to measure dry ingredients:

> **Measuring by volume:** Volume means how much space an ingredient occupies. It is one of the standard measurement techniques for dry ingredients. Cups, tbsp, tsp, and ounces are most commonly used volume units.

Tools for measuring by volume

If you want to measure your ingredients by volume, have a pair of dry measuring cups, four-cup i.e. one-quart measure, and a set of measuring spoons.

Dry measuring cups:

One quart or 4-cup measure:

Measuring spoons- 1/4tsp, ½ tsp, 1 tsp, ½ tbsp, and 1 tbsp:

Below table shows equivalencies for volume measurements:

A measure(in standard U.S. units)	Equivalency
1 tsp	5 ml
1 tbsp	3 tsp or 15 ml
¼ cup	4 tbsp or 59 ml
½ cup	8 tbsp or 118 ml
1 cup	16 tbsp or 237 ml
1 pint	2 cups or 473 ml
1 quart	2 pints or 946 ml(1 liter approx)

Dry ingredients like coconut flour, nuts, seeds, and cocoa powder should preferably be measured in measuring cups.
Sifting, scooping, and spooning are a few ways to measure such ingredients. The method by which you fill a measuring cup can greatly vary the weight of the ingredient under measurement.

So, the best technique is the "dip and sweep". It is explained below.

- All you need to do is to dip your measuring cup into the ingredient container and fill it up with some ingredient overflowing.
- Use a knife to level the ingredient at the top of the cup and let the extra fall off from the sides.
- The level of the ingredient should be at par with the brim of the measuring cup.

Let us see the equivalents of few known ingredients that we shall be using in our keto recipes.

Measure(volume)	Equivalencies(mass)
1 cup all purpose flour	5 ounces 148 grams
1 cup cocoa powder	3 ounces 89 grams

1 cup coconut flour	3.95 ounces 128 grams
1 cup nuts	5 ounces150 grams
1 cup seeds	5.08 ounces 152.16 grams

> ➤ **Measuring by weight:** It is another convenient way to measure dry ingredients in which you can measure everything in the same bowl placed on a weighing scale.

The steps to measure by weight are listed below.

Suppose you want to cook a keto pancake that requires 22.5 ounces of coconut flour, 0.5 ounces of Stevia, and 0.35 ounces of yeast as dry ingredients.

- You will first place the mixing bowl on the scale and make sure the reading shows "0". Then start adding flour into it till it shows 22.5 ounces. Take out and set aside.
- Measure other ingredients in a similar way.

This is also a reliable way to measure dry ingredients. For your keto diet, you should know beforehand what you are going to cook. Keep your dry ingredients measured in advance and ready. After all, you do not want to consume less or more grams of any ingredient unknowingly.

6. Marinate Fish and Meat Overnight

Since keto is on, let us make it more beneficial by marinating and grilling our fish and meat. This is a very easy way to cook with minimum nutrition loss.

Let me explain to you why you should marinate your fish, meat, and chicken when you are going keto.

- Marinating fish, poultry, and meat largely restrict the production of Heterocyclic Amines (HA). These are carcinogenic chemical produced when meat is cooked at a high temperature. Marination lowers the production of HC to almost 99%.
- The acidic nature of marinades prevents the growth of gut-irritating bacteria like listeria. Having a healthy gut is great when you are in ketosis.
- Using reduced sugar marinades while cooking a meat steak, chicken breasts, and fish provides you with an almost carb-free, ample protein, and high-fat keto meal. Chicken with skin on, meat ribs, and fatty fish are a great option for a keto dish.
- Marinations renders the meat, fish, and chicken tender. Thus, the protein becomes easy to digest and you are able to get the amino acids you need when you are in ketosis.
- It helps in retaining the moisture of the meat.
- It also helps in lowering the calorie intake. A little marinade is enough to coat a bowl of meat and so the excess intake is avoided. Make sure your marinade has reduced carbs. I prefer homemade marinades for a ketogenic diet.
- Always put the marinated meat in the fridge. That helps in complete elimination of harmful bacteria.
- Immediately use the marinade you prepare. If anything is from it, boil it along to kill bacteria.
- Consume the marinated fish and poultry within 2 days of marination and meat within 5.

How to marinate meat, fish, and chicken for a keto dish?

- If you are marinating meat then choose a fatty cut of meat like the ribs.
- Defrost it by placing it in an air-tight container in the fridge.
- Make deep cuts into it and place it into a glass bowl.
- Make your marinade by mixing lemon juice, olive oil, crushed garlic, rosemary, pepper, salt, bay leaf, mixed spices, and sugar-free sauce.
- Pour it on the meat and make sure all the sides of the meat are coated well with the marinade.
- Place it in the fridge for at least 8 hours or overnight before cooking.

The process remains the same for chicken and meat. You should preferably marinate a chicken that has skin on. Chicken skin contains a lot of fats. For fish, marinate a fatty fish as it contains plenty of Omega 3-fatty acids. Don't marinate fish for more than 3 hours.

7. Make Condiments for Yourself

Making condiments at home is great if you want to go keto. The reason is that the condiments that are available in the market have hidden carb content not notified on the label.

Don't be fooled by the low-carb or carb-free label. Instead, make condiments at home and that too with reduced carbs or carb-free.

1st. Keto chili alioli:

Net Carbs: 1 gram/serving
Fats: 46grams
Proteins: 1gram
Calories: 413kcl
Ingredients:
- 1 egg
- 2 garlic cloves
- ¾ cup avocado oil
- ½ tsp chili flakes and salt
- ¼ tsp pepper
- 1 tbsp lime juice
- 3 tbsp Greek yogurt

Preparation:

➢ Beat garlic and egg in a bowl.
➢ Add oil in small quantities and keep whisking vigorously till it emulsifies.
➢ Beat yogurt and spices and add to the emulsified mixture.
➢ Mix well and store in a glass jar in the fridge.

2nd. Butter mayonnaise

Net Carbs: 0.3grams/serving
Fat: 32 grams
Proteins: 1 gram
Calories: 285kcl
Ingredients:
- 5 ½ ounces butter
- 1 egg
- 1 tbsp Dijon mustard

- 1 tsp lime juice
- Salt and pepper

Preparation:

➢ Melt the butter and transfer to a jug to cool it down.
➢ Beat eggs and mustard in a bowl and pour the butter over it.
➢ Whisk vigorously till it emulsifies.
➢ Add salt, pepper, and lime juice and spoon out in a glass jar.
➢ Store in the fridge.

3rd. Hollandaise sauce

Net Carbs: 1 grams/serving
Fats: 65grmas
Proteins: 3grams
Calories: 594
Ingredients:
- 4 egg yolks
- 2 tbsp mustard sauce
- 10 ounces butter
- Salt and pepper

Preparation:

➢ Melt the butter and whisk the yolks.
➢ Add the molten butter drop by drop to the yolks while beating vigorously till the mixture emulsifies.
➢ Add sauce, salt, and pepper and store in a jar.

4th. Flavored water

Net Carbs: 0
Fats: 0
Proteins: 0
Calories: 0
Ingredients:
- 4 cups fresh water
- Flavors such as raspberry, mint, or cucumber

- 2 cups ice cube

Preparation:

> ➤ Add cold water to a pitcher and add the flavor of your choice like cucumber slices, 1/2 cup berries, juice and zest of 1 orange, etc. to it and leave undisturbed for 30 minutes.
> ➤ This will flavor the entire pitcher.
> ➤ Store the flavored water in a jar.

5th. Spicy keto pimiento cheese

Net Carbs: 1 grams/serving
Fats: 24grams
Proteins: 7grams
Calories: 246kcal
Ingredients:
- 15 tsp mayonnaise
- 4 tbsp chopped pimientos
- 1 tsp paprika powder
- 1 tbsp Dijon mustard
- 1 pinch cayenne pepper
- 4 ounces cheddar cheese shredded
- 1 tbsp chopped chives

Preparation:

> ➤ Thoroughly mix all the ingredients excluding chive and refrigerate for 2 hours.
> ➤ Make small balls from it and top each ball with chives.
> ➤ Store in glass jars and use with your favorite keto meal.

There are many other condiments that you can make at home. Hit the internet and discover a few other easy low-carb condiment recipes.

8. Using pressure cooker

When you start a keto diet, it is a different experience. You have to bid goodbye to the foods you have been eating for long and adapt to a different menu where tracking of your carbs, proteins, and fats is important.

One kitchen appliance that is tremendously helpful in a keto kitchen is a pressure cooker or an instant pot.

There are plenty of benefits of using a pressure cooker to cook keto meals such as:

> Pressure cooker or instant pot helps you too cook several hundreds of varieties especially meat in very less time in its typical "set and forget style".
> It is ideal for a keto dieter for meal planning, quick recipes, and especially for the one who has less expertise in oven and stove cooking.
> As a keto dieter, all you need to do is to learn a few quick instant pot recipes especially with meat, beef, or chicken, and stuffing your pantry with the required ingredients.
> Pressure cooker cooking works wonders with a restrictive keto dieter.
> Slow cooking keto recipes like bone broth and various soups that take more than 7 hours to cook are best made in a pressure cooker or an instant pot.
> Pressure cooker cooking helps save a lot of time. It is almost 30% quick that any other traditional cooking style.
> As the food is cooked fast, most of the nutrients, vitamins, and minerals are retained. For a keto dieter, this is very helpful in maintaining good health, hormonal level, and a healthy gut.

In the last part of the book, I will discuss a few easy and delicious instant pot keto recipes that you can try. For now, remember to buy one for yourself. It will be your best kitchen pal in the keto meal journey.

9. Make Bone Broth, Chicken Stock or Vegetable Stock

You consume a lot of meat when you are on a keto diet and that comes with its own set of drawbacks. But the good news is that there is an excellent solution to this problem known as the bone broth. Bone broth makes the meat protein healthier, cancer-free, and better.

The keto diet is better with a bone broth. Below are a few marvelous benefits of bone broth:

> Bone broth is very satisfying. You should have it for a filled stomach while you are on a Ketogenic diet.
> It contains plenty of collagen which is great for restoring and increasing muscle mass.
> It detoxifies the body.
> It is very gut-friendly.
> It helps in dealing with joint pain.

> ➤ It is a great anti-inflammatory agent.

You can very conveniently make it at home and store it in your fridge. It can also be used in different recipes of the keto diet. Check below to see how to make it at home.

1st. Bone Broth

Net carbs: 0.7 grams
Proteins: 3.6 grams
Fat: 6 grams
Calories: 72kcal
Serving: 6-8 cups
Ingredients:

- 1.5 kg of mixed bones of beef and marrow
- 2 carrots
- 1 parsley root
- 2 celery stalks
- 1 onion
- 5 peeled garlic cloves
- 3 bay leaves
- 1 tbsp pink Himalayan salt
- 8-10 cups water

Preparation:

> ➤ Chop the vegetables and put into a pressure cooker along with bay leaves.
> ➤ Add bones to it.
> ➤ Pour water into it along with a generous squeeze of lemon.
> ➤ Add a dash of Himalayan salt.
> ➤ Close the lid of the pressure cooker and cook on high flame for 10 minutes and then on a slow flame for 90 minutes.
> ➤ Once done, let the pressure release naturally and open the lid.
> ➤ Pass the contents through a strainer.
> ➤ Discard the vegetables and bay leaves and strip the meat off from the bones using a fork.
> ➤ Preserve the bones with gelatin on for next bone broth preparation.
> ➤ Store the broth in a glass jar in your fridge.

2nd. Chicken stock

Keep chicken stock prepared in advance. It will be used in different recipes of your keto diet plan.

Net carbs: 0.4 grams
Proteins: 2.8 grams
Fat: 5 grams
Calories: 57kcal
Serving: 8 cups

Ingredients:

- 13 pounds of chicken back and wings
- 4 chopped celery stalks
- 4 chopped carrots
- 1 quartered onion
- 6 peeled garlic cloves
- 1 cup fresh parsley
- 1 tsp dried thyme
- 1 tsp kosher salt
- 4 quarts cold water

Preparation:

➢ Assemble all the ingredients in a pot and bring to boil.
➢ Reduce heat and cook for 2 hours till the chicken bones turn tender and fall apart.
➢ Once done, pass it through a strainer and squeeze the contents to extract maximum broth.
➢ Discard the squeezed contents and store the broth in an air-tight glass jar in your fridge.

3rd. Vegetable stock

Vegetable stock can be used as an ingredient of many keto recipes. It is always better that you make it at home and store in your fridge.
If you have prepared beef broth or chicken broth, I advise you to use that over vegetable stock because they have a higher protein and fat value as compared to vegetable stock. They also contain less carbs.
Here is the recipe of vegetable stock.

Net carbs: 3 grams
Proteins: 0.2 grams

Fat: 0.5 grams
Calories: 12kcal
Serving: 5 cups
Ingredients:

- 2 onions
- 3 carrots
- 4 celery stalks
- 5 sprigs of thyme
- 1 bay leaf
- 1 bunch of parsley
- 1 tsp whole peppercorns
- 1 bowl mixed leeks, fennel, tomatoes, mushrooms, and parsnips
- 1 tsp kosher salt
- 4 cups water

Preparation:

- ➤ Chop and wash all the vegetables and place in a pressure cooker.
- ➤ Pour the water and bring the contents to boil.
- ➤ Close the lid and let a few wisps of the steam pass.
- ➤ Lower the flame and cook for 1.5 hours.
- ➤ Pass the vegetables through a strainer and squeeze to take out the maximum liquid.
- ➤ Discard the vegetables and preserve the stock in a glass jar in the fridge.

10. Purposing Leftovers

How many times have you discovered a bowl or container of food in your fridge that has been lying there for weeks completely forgotten? Don't feel guilty. You are not alone.

But as now you have realized it, isn't it great to purpose the leftover food for all good reasons like financial, social, and environmental? This scenario is especially true for a keto diet.

In Keto diet, you will find a lot of leftover food. No! You are not going to throw it; rather you will purpose it in a way that it can be conveniently used in the next meal. In this section, I will explain how you can purpose your leftover food:

- ✓ **Plan your leftovers:** Select your keto meal in advance and think of all the extras you can get at the end. This will give you an idea of how to utilize those extras. Suppose, you want to prepare beef bacon and vegetable salad for the dinner.

You must plan in advance that the extra vegetables can be straight used in the soup for the lunch next day or in the week. Similarly, leftover shredded chicken is a great idea for a chicken salad.

- ✓ **Store leftovers smartly:** Glass containers are an amazing way to store leftovers. Label the container with date and contents stored. This makes the task easy and you won't lose track. If you want to freeze something like gelatin containing bones for a next bone broth batch, then use Ziploc bags.
- ✓ **Select a leftover meal:** Dedicate a meal entirely to finish the leftovers. Like you have some roasted salmon, some salad, and soup leftover in the fridge. So, today's dinner should be a vegetable salad with roasted salmon sandwich and soup.
- ✓ **Yesterday's dinner is today's lunch:** A nice way to save money and time is to consume yesterday's dinner as lunch for the next day. You might need to make something extra, but the leftover food will be utilized effectively.
  If you have some leftover meat, drizzle some olive oil on it, place a thick slice of cheese, a slice of tomato, salt, and pepper and bake it. Enjoy a lovely snack full of proteins.
- ✓ **Convert leftover foods into ingredients:** cooked veggies can be blended with fresh tomatoes into a nice sauce. Extra pasta can make a nice frittata. Leftover meat and veggies are suitable ingredients for burritos.
- ✓ **Make soup:** The leftover chicken and vegetables can be blended into a nice soup with some chicken stock and a dash of salt and pepper.
- ✓ **Stash meat, chicken and vegetable leftovers:** make a nice broth from the leftovers of meat, chicken, beef, or vegetables.
- ✓ **Create a kitchen sink:** if you have cheese, steak, shrimp, or chicken leftovers, cook them with some lettuce or baby spinach into a nice dressing.
- ✓ **Portion before storing:** divide a big loaf of beef or meat, a large-sized fatty fish, or a large brick of cheese into small packets before freezing. You can use one packet at a time.
- ✓ Store veggies and meat separately and mix them on the dinner plates.
- ✓ Mix and match your leftovers to create unique dishes. Like a portion of leftover minced meat with some salad and mustard sauce makes a yummy lunch.
- ✓ Eat salads. Combine leftover veggies with a heavy fat and protein source like leftover steak, chicken, pork chops, boiled eggs, salmon, cheese, tuna, and nuts. Drizzle your favorite dressing, herbs, and sour cream. Enjoy.

11. Meal Prepping in Advance

This is no extra work. Rather, weekly meal prep helps to make your keto diet a success. It also helps in saving energy, time, and money.

In this section, I will cover how to prep for a keto meal.

How to start keto meal prep

With all the things in the right place and handy, your cooking will become easy and hassle-free. There are some basic pieces of equipment you need to have in your kitchen when you want to prepare a keto meal. I have already discussed the essential ingredients in the "keto staples" section of this chapter.

Equipment of a keto meal

Most of these are already present in your kitchen; however, you might need to buy a few.

EQUIPMENT YOU NEED FOR MEAL PREP

SKILLET

QUALITY CHEF'S KNIFE

FOOD PROCESSOR OR BLENDER

SLOW COOKER OR CROCKPOT

PARCHMENT PAPER

GLASS FOOD CONTAINERS

OTHER HELPFUL BUT NOT NECESSARY TOOLS

IMMERSION BLENDER

VEGETABLE SPIRALIZER

KITCHEN SCALE

- **Skillet:** consider buying skillets of different sizes if possible. If not, at least buy one of a good quality.
- **Chef's knife:** a good quality chef's knife is necessary. You may need to do a lot of chopping and slicing.
- **Food processor:** food processor will enable you to try hundreds of different recipes. It will also save a lot of time. If you can't afford one, then buy a blender instead.
- **Cook pot:** known as the "set and forget device", it is an absolutely grand gadget in your kitchen. You just throw your stuff into it and see the magic it does while you are engaged in other works.
- **Parchment paper:** to prevent sticking when you bake, parchment paper is a good idea. It is cheap as well.
- **Air-tight glass containers**: glass is microwave safe and better than plastic containers. You can divide the meals into servings in different glass jars and grab one when you need.
- **Other helpful but not necessary equipment**: immersion blender, vegetable spiralizer, and kitchen scale are also useful in a keto kitchen. Buy if you can, if you can't, it is ok.

Go to the nearby store and grab the keto ingredients and tools. You are going to use them all very soon.

3 steps for an easy keto meal prep
The diagram below illustrates the general structure for an easy meal prep.

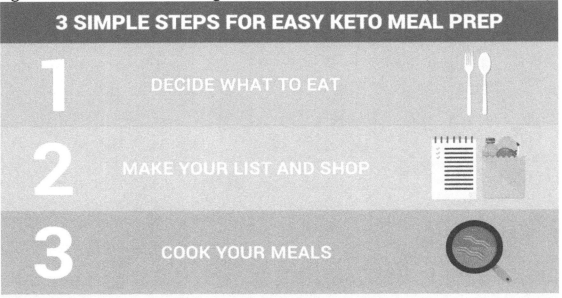

3 SIMPLE STEPS FOR EASY KETO MEAL PREP

1 DECIDE WHAT TO EAT

2 MAKE YOUR LIST AND SHOP

3 COOK YOUR MEALS

PERFECT KETO

- **1. Decide what to eat**: select a day in a week and plan in advance what you want to eat for the coming seven days. This will include points like:
  - ✓ What shall be the breakfast, lunch, dinner, snacks, and desserts menu for each day of the week? Have a count of the carbs, fats, and protein value of each recipe.
  - ✓ How many serving you will cook and how are you going to purpose the leftovers of each meal.
  - ✓ Have the same meal more than once a week. That way you will be able to save time and you can also utilize the leftovers.
  - ✓ Know the recipes and ingredients required in each in advance.
  - ✓ Decide when to buy the ingredients and when to cook the meals.

- **2. Make Your List and Shop:** After selecting your weekly menu, it is time to go for some shopping. Keep the following points in mind:
  - ✓ Make a detailed list of the ingredients.
  - ✓ Know the exact amount of each ingredient you need.
  - ✓ Buy real and whole foods.
  - ✓ Avoid buying refined and processed stuff and don't trust the "low-carb or no-carb" label.

- **3. Cook Your Meals:** Now, this is time for some real action. Don't worry if things don't work out the first time. Practice will make you perfect.

Consider the following tips:

- ✓ Thoroughly read the recipes and take the longest step first e.g. if you want to cook a slow-cooker chicken, then, washing and chopping the veggies should be your first course of action.
- ✓ Have all the ingredients including broth, condiments, and frozen stuff handy.
- ✓ If there are some steps like pre-preparing meat pre-chopping veggies, then do it in advance. This step will help you save a lot of time when you start cooking.
- ✓ Once cooked, divide the meals in separate air-tight containers before refrigerating.

This brings an end to the preparation section of your keto diet journey. Before we take up the recipes, let me make you aware regarding the food choices you can make when you take up the keto diet. There are some foods you should eat abundantly and some you should avoid. The coming chapter focuses on your keto food list.

Chapter 6- Complete Keto Diet Food List

When you plan to go keto and enter the grocery store for the first time to do some keto shopping, no wonder you will be lost and confused. What should I buy? What can I eat? Is that food too carb-rich? I hope this food contains enough fats? How about proteins? All these questions will make it difficult for you to make a choice.

To make things easier for you, I have divided this chapter into three parts. What to eat, what to avoid, and some advice on drinks.

So, let me begin with foods that you are allowed to eat.

What to Eat

Here is a detailed list of the foods you should eat. I have classified the foods into various categories like vegetables, dairy, meat, etc.

Please bear in mind that few foods can be higher in carbs like carrots. So simply remember, whatever tastes sweet should be consumed less.

> **Vegetables: Eat veggies in bulk especially greens. Avoid root veggies.**

- Artichokes
- Asparagus
- Bok Choy
- Broccoli
- Brussels Sprouts
- Butterhead Lettuce
- Cabbage
- Cauliflower
- Celery
- Chicory Greens
- Chives
- Cucumber
- Eggplant

- Fennel
- Garlic
- Kale
- Leeks
- Leafy Greens (Various)
- Lettuce
- Mushrooms (all kinds)
- Mustard Greens
- Okra
- Onions
- Parsley
- Pumpkin
- Radicchio

- Radishes
- Romaine Lettuce
- Scallion
- Shallots
- Seaweed (all sea vegetables)
- Shallots
- Spinach
- Tomatoes
- Turnip Greens
- Watercress
- Zucchini

Fermented Vegetables
- Kimchi
- Sauerkraut

> **Fruits: Most fruits are not allowed on a keto diet. A few that are allowed are listed below.**

- Avocado
- Blackberry
- Blueberry
- Cranberry
- Lemon
- Lime
- Olive
- Raspberry
- Strawberry

> **Meat: Have fatty cuts of meat and watch your protein and fat intake.**

- Beef
- Bison
- Chicken
- Deer
- Duck
- Goat
- Goose
- Lamb
- Pork
- Reindeer
- Sheep
- Turkey

Prepared meat (check ingredients)

- Sausages
- Hot Dogs
- Pepperoni
- Salami
- Bacon

Organ meat

- Bone Marrow
- Heart
- Kidney
- Liver
- Tongue

> **Legumes: Legumes are off limits except these two.**

- Green Beans
- Peas

> **Fats: You should take plenty of fats from the right sources like:**

- Avocado Oil
- Cocoa Butter
- Coconut Oil
- Duck Fat
- Ghee
- Lard (non-hydrogenated)
- MCT Oil
- Olive Oil
- Red Palm Oil
- Sesame Oil (small amounts)
- Tallow
- Walnut Oil (small amounts)

> **Fish: Fish is very rich in omega 3-fatty acids.**

- Bass
- Cod
- Eel
- Haddock
- Halibut
- Herring
- Mackerel
- Perch
- Red Snapper
- Rockfish
- Salmon
- Sardines
- Tuna (including Albacore)
- Turbot
- Trout

> **Other seafood: These are also a rich source of nutrition.**

- Abalone
- Clams
- Crab
- Lobster
- Oysters
- Shrimp
- Scallops
- Squid

> **Nuts and seeds: Watch your nut intake. They are easy to munch and you may over-eat.**

- Almonds
- Hazelnuts
- Pecans
- Pistachios
- Pumpkin Seeds
- Sesame Seeds
- Sunflower Seeds
- Walnuts
- Cashews
- Chia Seeds
- Various Nut Butters
- Hemp Seeds

> **Herbs and spices: Use the following herbs and spices for a delicious keto meal.**

- Sea Salt
- Black Pepper
- White Pepper
- Basil
- Italian Seasoning
- Chili Powder
- Cayenne Pepper
- Curry Powder
- Cumin
- Oregano
- Thyme
- Rosemary
- Sage
- Turmeric
- Parsley
- Cilantro/Coriander
- Cinnamon
- Nutmeg
- Cloves
- Ginger
- Cardamom
- Paprika
- Dill

> **Dairy: Eat the following dairy products in abundance.**
- Ghee
- Eggs
- Cheese (all kinds)

> **Other foods you should eat**

- Mayonnaise (homemade)
- Coconut Butter
- Beef Jerky
- Pickles
- Cod Liver Oil (Fish Oil)
- Cacao Powder (unsweetened)
- Vinegar (with no added sugar)
- Shredded Coconut
- Mustard
- Hot Sauce (check ingredients)
- Vanilla Extract
- Coconut Flour
- Tamari Sauce (Gluten-Free)
- Coconut Aminos
- Fish Sauce (check ingredients)
- Gelatin (as a powder or from bone broth)
- 100% Dark Chocolate
- Stevia (only small amounts)
- Monk Fruit

- Almond Flour

What to Avoid

Knowing what to avoid in a keto diet is absolutely as important as knowing what to eat. There are a few foods you should avoid while you are on a keto diet. Otherwise, your whole process of ketosis can be rendered worthless.

➢ **Sugars: Sugar in any form is completely off limits. Here is a list.**

- White Sugar
- Fructose
- Corn Syrup
- Dextrose
-

- Honey
- Glucose
- Maple Syrup
- Maltose

- Agave
- Coconut Sugar
- Brown Sugar
- Lactose

➢ **Grains: Grains are carb-rich and thus off limits. Please don't buy the following.**

- Wheat
- White Flour
- Quinoa
- Rye
- Couscous
- All purpose flours

- Rice
- Wheat Flour
- Oats
- Barley
- Cornmeal
- Corn

- Rice Flour
- Millet
- Bran
- Buckwheat

➢ **Processed foods: These have hidden carbs and not at all keto-friendly. A strict no to the followings foods.**

- Bread
- Potato Chips
- Ice Cream
- Waffles
- Candy
- Crackers

- Tortilla Chips
- Pretzels
- Pancakes
- Ketchup
- Dressing
- Cookies

- Baked Goods
- Snack Bars
- Cereal
- Most Sauces

➢ **Fruits: Almost all the fruits are rich in carbs. So, they are not allowed on a keto diet.**

- Canned Fruit
- Apples
- Oranges
- Pears
- Peaches
- Pomegranate

- Nectarines
- Grapes
- Watermelon
- Cantaloupe
- Kiwi
- Date

- Bananas
- Cherries
- Mangos
- Apricot
- Papaya
- Fig

➢ **Legumes: Avoid all legumes except peas and green beans. Below is a list of the legumes you should not purchase.**

- All beans
- Lentils
- Soybeans

➢ **Low-carb foods: A low-carb food doesn't necessarily qualify to be a keto food. Avoid the following foods.**

- Sugar Alcohols
- Blue Cheese Salad Dressing
- Canola, Sunflower Seed, and other seed or vegetable oils
- Artificial Sweeteners (erythritol, Splenda, sucralose, etc.)
- Low carb gluten-containing foods
- Peanut butter
- Diet Sodas
- Soy products (soy milk, tofu)

Advice of Drink

Drinks demand special attention because they are more prone to have hidden carbohydrates. So, before you select a drink, carefully check its nutritional information particularly with respect to cab content.
The list provided below will definitely help you to make some good drink choices.

Drinks you should have: **You can have these drinks but don't forget to pick the unsweetened one.**
- Almond Milk
- Broth (chicken, beef, vegetable, bone)
- Cashew Milk
- Club Soda

- Coconut Milk (Unsweetened)
- Unsweetened Coffee
- Herbal Teas
- Lemon and Lime Juice (small amounts)
- Seltzer Water
- Sparkling Mineral Water
- Unsweetened Tea
- Water
- Electrolytes

> **Drinks you should avoid**: **The following drinks have high carb content. Avoid all of these or they can bring you out of ketosis easily.**

- Sodas
- Sports Drinks
- Juices
- All Alcohols
- Milk
- Sweetened Tea or Coffee

Before I move to the recipes section, I want you to go through this checklist and tick-mark the following points. If there is any point you have missed, finish that task immediately.

Check the following points:

- ☑ I have a thorough concept of ketosis and how it works.
- ☑ I know how to track my macros.
- ☑ I know how to extract the nutritional information of the meals.
- ☑ I know the do's and don'ts of ketosis.
- ☑ I am aware of keto flu.
- ☑ My keto staples, equipment, and ingredients are ready.
- ☑ I have done the keto prepping.
- ☑ I know how to purpose the leftovers.
- ☑ I have measured ingredients in advance.
- ☑ My homemade keto condiments are ready in advance.
- ☑ I have frozen berries and herbs.
- ☑ I have parboiled and frozen my veggies.
- ☑ I have prepared bone broth, chicken and vegetable stock.
- ☑ I have marinated chicken, meat, and fish.
- ☑ I have purchased a nice instant pot or pressure cooker.

If you have tick-marked all of the above points, it means that you are ready for some real action. In the coming chapters, I will discuss some delicious keto meal ideas with you that you can try your hands on.

Part 2: Simple Keto Recipes

Chapter 7- Keto breakfast and lunch delights

Dear readers, it is time to roll up your sleeves and put on your chef's hat because in this chapter you are going to try some mouth-watering keto breakfast and lunch recipes that you can include into your daily menu.

Delicious keto breakfasts

1. Keto brunch spread

Net carbs: 3grams
Proteins: 17grams
Fats: 38grams
Calories: 426 kcal
Serving size: 4
Ingredients:

- 4 eggs
- 24 asparagus spears
- 12 slices bacon

Preparation:

➢ Preheat the oven to 400F.
➢ Wrap bacon slices firmly on each spear.
➢ Bake for 20 minutes.
➢ Boil the eggs for 6 minutes and remove the shell.
➢ Serve the asparagus-bacon spears with eggs.

2. Keto power breakfast

Net carbs: 5grams
Proteins: 10.6grams
Fats: 27.4grams
Calories: 305 kcal
Serving size: 2

Ingredients:

- 1 cup baby spinach, arugula, parsley, and olive oil
- 5 garlic cloves
- 5 tbsp hemp seeds
- 5 bacon slices
- 2 eggs
- 20 asparagus spears
- Salt and pepper

Preparation:

- ➢ Pulse the vegetables, hemp seeds, and olive oil into a thick sauce and set aside. Arrange bacon slices in a ring shape on a pan.
- ➢ Place 4 asparagus tips in each ring and crack an egg.
- ➢ Bake for 20 minutes and serve.

3. Keto breakfast tacos

Net carbs: 4grams
Proteins: 20grams
Fats: 29grams
Calories: 360 kcal
Serving size: 1

Ingredients:

- 3 oz shredded cheddar cheese
- 1 egg
- 2 slices mutton
- 2 cilantro sprigs
- 1 tbsp arugula
- 1 tsp butter
- Salt and pepper

Preparation:

- ➢ Fry the meat till brown.
- ➢ Melt the cheese in a circle on a pan.
- ➢ Crack an egg in the cheese circle.
- ➢ Sprinkle salt and pepper on the yolk.
- ➢ Cook for 4 minutes.
- ➢ Place the cheese-egg, meat, arugula, and cilantro in a taco and serve.

4. Energizing keto smoothie

Net carbs: 4grams
Proteins: 8grams
Fats: 26grams
Calories: 250 kcal
Serving size: 1

Ingredients:

- 1 cup cashew milk
- 1 tbsp keto MCT oil
- 1 tbsp keto nut butter
- 2 tbsp maca powder
- Few ice cubes

Preparation:

➢ Assemble all the ingredients in a food processor and pulse into a thick smoothie.
➢ Serve immediately.

5. Keto collagen chocolate smoothie

Net carbs: 2.2grams
Proteins: 13.6grams
Fats: 49.4grams
Calories: 500 kcal
Serving size: 1

Ingredients:

- ½ avocado
- 2 scoops keto chocolate collagen
- 1 tbsp soaked chia seeds
- 1 tbsp almond butter
- ¾ cup heavy whipping cream
- 1 ½ cup water
- Few ice cubes

Preparation:

➢ Throw all the ingredients into a food processor and pulse for 2 minutes into a thick smoothie.
➢ Serve.

6. Salmon keto avocado toast

Net carbs: 6grams
Proteins: 22grams
Fats: 33grams
Calories: 418 kcal
Serving size: 2

Ingredients:

- 1 tbsp butter
- 2 slices almond flour bread
- 2 oz smoked salmon
- ½ avocado
- 1 sliced cucumber
- ½ tsp red pepper flakes, salt, pepper, dill, and chopped capers
- 1 tbsp sliced onion

Preparation:

- Apply butter on the bread slices and toast till brown.
- Place mashed avocado on each slide.
- Add salt, pepper, and pepper flakes.
- Arrange cucumber and salmon slices on each toast.
- Garnish with capers, dill, and onions. Serve.

7. Matcha latte flourless pancakes

Net carbs: 7.6grams
Proteins: 14.6grams
Fats: 38.9grams
Calories: 418 kcal
Serving size: 3

Ingredients:

- 2 tbsp nut butter
- 2 scoops keto MCT powder
- 1 egg
- ¼ cup blueberries
- 1 tbsp butter

Preparation:

- Combine the nut butter, egg, and MCT powder in a smooth paste.
- Coat a large skillet with oil and pour the batter on it in round shape.
- Disperse a few blueberries on each pancake.
- Cook on both sides for 3 minutes and serve.

8. Keto oatmeal

Net carbs: 8.2grams
Proteins: 31grams
Fats: 44grams

Calories: 584 kcal
Serving size: 1

Ingredients:

- 1 cup unsweetened almond milk
- ½ cup hemp hearts
- 1 tbsp flax seeds, chia seeds, and coconut flakes
- 1 tsp cinnamon powder
- 1 scoop vanilla flavored MCT oil powder
- 1 cup frozen blueberries

Preparation:

- ➢ Stir-combine all the ingredients in a pot.
- ➢ Cook on low flame till you get your desired consistency.
- ➢ Top with frozen blueberries and serve.

9. Instant pot keto Lasagna

Net carbs: 4grams
Proteins: 25grams
Fats: 25grams

Calories: 365 kcal
Serving size: 8

Ingredients:

- 1 pound minced beef
- 2 minced garlic cloves
- 1 onion
- 1 ½ cup ricotta cheese
- 1 ½ cup Parmesan cheese
- 1 egg
- 25 ounces marinara sauce
- 8 ounces sliced mozzarella

Preparation:

- ➢ Cook beef, garlic, and onion in the instant pot.
- ➢ Blend cheese and egg in a bowl.
- ➢ Drain the liquid from the beef and add the sauce.
- ➢ Spread a layer of the mozzarella cheese on the beef, followed by a layer of the cheese-egg mixture, followed by more sauce.
- ➢ Repeat the layers once again.
- ➢ Cover with an aluminum foil.
- ➢ Pour a cup of water into the pot and place the dish over a rack in the pot.
- ➢ Cook for 10 minutes.
- ➢ Remove the foil and spoon the lasagna into bowls. Serve.

10. Instant pot keto cheese frittata

Net carbs: 5grams
Proteins: 14grams
Fats: 19grams
Calories: 257 kcal
Serving size: 8

Ingredients:

- 4 eggs
- 10-ounce green chiles
- Salt
- ½ tsp cumin powder
- 1 cup shredded Mexican cheese

Preparation:

- ➢ Combine all the ingredients in a bowl.
- ➢ Pour the mixture into a pan and cover with an aluminum foil.
- ➢ Cook on high-pressure in your instant pot for 20 minutes.
- ➢ Take the foil off and scatter more cheese on the top.
- ➢ Place under a broiler till the cheese melts. Serve.

Yummy keto lunch delights

11. White turkey chili

Net carbs: 5.5grams
Proteins: 30.5grams
Fats: 19grams
Calories: 388 kcal
Serving size: 5

Ingredients:

- 1 lb ground turkey
- 2 cups cauliflower rice
- 2 tbsp coconut oil
- ½ minced onion
- 2 minced garlic cloves
- 2 cups coconut milk(full-fat)
- 1 tbsp mustard
- 1 tsp thyme, garlic, and pepper powder
- Salt

Preparation:

- ➢ Sauté onion and garlic in some oil and cook till brown.
- ➢ Add turkey and cook till done.
- ➢ Add the cauliflower rice, spice mix, and coconut milk.
- ➢ Cook on low flame for 10 minutes. Serve.

12. BBQ beef Sando

Net carbs: 2grams
Proteins: 5.1grams
Fats: 15.1grams
Calories: 184 kcal
Serving size: 4
Ingredients:

- 2 beef loaves
- 2 tsp salt and garlic powder
- 1 tsp onion powder
- Salt
- Pepper

- 1 tbsp paprika
- 2 tbsp tomato paste and coconut aminos
- ¼ cup butter
- ½ cup bone broth

Preparation:

➢ Mix the spices and rub on the beef loaves.
➢ Combine molten butter, tomato paste, bone broth, and coconut aminos into a paste.
➢ Pour it over the beef and cook for 10-12 hours to make a thick sauce. Serve.

13. Keto meat roll

Net carbs: 4grams
Proteins: 33grams
Fats: 29grams
Calories: 184 kcal
Serving size: 6
Ingredients:

- 2 pounds minced beef
- ½ tsp Himalayan salt
- ¼ cup yeast, parsley, and oregano

- Salt and pepper
- 2 eggs
- 2 tbsp avocado oil
- 4 garlic cloves

Preparation:

➢ Preheat the oven to 400F. Combine the beef with salt, pepper, and yeast.
➢ Pulse the eggs, garlic, herbs, and oil into a smooth blend.
➢ Pour the blend on the beef and combine.
➢ Bake for 1 hour. Drain the extra liquid and serve.

14. Super-food meatballs

Net carbs: 4.3grams
Proteins: 31.8grams
Fats: 35grams
Calories: 323 kcal
Serving size: 10

Ingredients:

- 3 lbs ground mutton
- 4 chopped shallots and carrots
- 3 garlic cloves
- 1 tbsp herbs

- 2 tbsp coconut aminos
- Salt
- Olive oil

Preparation:

- ➢ Sauté the vegetables till soft.
- ➢ Add meat and remaining ingredients and cook till the meat turns brown.
- ➢ Transfer to a mixer and pulse.
- ➢ Make balls from the mixture and place on a sheet pan.
- ➢ Preheat the oven to 425F.
- ➢ Bake for 20 minutes and serve.

15. Shrimp keto stir-fry

Net carbs: 3.3grams
Proteins: 23.7grams
Fats: 24.8grams
Calories: 357kcal
Serving size: 4

Ingredients:

- 16oz peeled shrimp
- Chopped ginger root
- 4 chopped green onion stalks
- 2 minced garlic cloves

- 4 mushrooms
- 1 cup coconut aminos
- 2 tsp Himalayan salt
- 3 tbsp bacon fat

Preparation:

- ➢ Heat bacon fat in a pan and add the ginger root, onion, garlic, and mushrooms to it. Cook till tender.
- ➢ Add the shrimp, salt, and coconut aminos and cook till shrimp is pink. Serve.

16. Creamy keto fish casserole

Net carbs: 6grams
Proteins: 41grams
Fats: 69grams
Calories: 822kcal
Serving size: 4

Ingredients:

- 2 tbsp olive oil and capers
- 15 oz broccoli florets
- 6 scallions
- 1 tbsp parsley and mustard
- 25 oz salmon fish
- 1 ½ cup cream
- Salt
- Pepper
- 3 tbsp butter

Preparation:

- ➤ Preheat the oven to 400F. Fry broccoli florets, scallions, and capers till soft.
- ➤ Transfer the veggies and fish to a pan.
- ➤ Pour the whipping cream, parsley, salt, pepper and mustard over the contents and bake for 20 minutes. Serve.

17. Beef instant pot roast

Net carbs: 3grams
Proteins: 30grams
Fats: 28grams
Calories: 393kcal
Serving size: 10

Ingredients:

- 2 beef loaves
- Salt
- Pepper
- 1 tsp garlic powder
- ¼ cup vinegar
- 2 cups water
- 1 chopped onion

Preparation:

- ➤ Rub salt, pepper, and garlic powder on the beef loaves.
- ➤ Sauté the loaves and onion in instant pot till brown.
- ➤ Pour vinegar and water into it. Cook on high-pressure for 30 minutes.
- ➤ Transfer the beef to a bowl.
- ➤ Reduce the liquid to a thick sauce and add the beef back. Serve.

18. Instant pot Keto chicken chili

Net carbs: 5.3grams
Proteins: 23grams
Fats: 18grams

Calories: 306kcal
Serving size: 10

Ingredients:

- 2 lbs ground chicken
- 1 onion
- 8 garlic cloves
- 6 oz tomato paste
- 4 oz green chiles

- 2 tbsp keto chili aioli, cumin powder, and oregano
- ¼ cup chili powder
- Salt
- Pepper

Preparation:

- ➢ Sauté the onion and garlic in instant pot until soft.
- ➢ Add the minced chicken and cook till brown.
- ➢ Add all the ingredients and stir well.
- ➢ Select the stew setting and cook for 35 minutes. Serve.

19. Grilled lemon garlic fish

Net carbs: 2.7grams
Proteins: 27grams
Fats: 34grams

Calories: 293kcal
Serving size: 6

Ingredients:

- 1 bowl halibut fish

Marinade ingredients

- 1 tbsp olive oil and lemon juice
- Pepper
- Salt

- 2 tsp homemade seasoning and garlic paste
- 1 tsp dried basil

Preparation:

- ➢ Mix the marinade ingredients.
- ➢ Put the fish in a Ziploc bag and pour the marinade over it.
- ➢ Set in the fridge for 3 hours.
- ➢ Preheat the grill and arrange the fish on it.
- ➢ Grill on each side for 6 minutes. Serve.

20. Roasted chicken stacks

Net carbs: 4.8grams
Proteins: 33.7grams
Fats: 36.2grams
Calories: 369 kcal
Serving size: 5

Ingredients:

- 5 chicken breast
- 1 cabbage
- 5 prosciutto slices
- 3 tbsp coconut flour
- Salt
- Pepper
- 2 tbsp mixed herbs
- ½ cup bone broth
- ¼ cup avocado oil

Preparation:

- Preheat the oven to 400F.
- Combine chicken breasts, oil, salt, pepper, herbs, and coconut flour in a Ziploc bag.
- Shred the cabbage and divide it into 5 piles on a baking sheet.
- Arrange the chicken and prosciutto slice on each pile.
- Roast for 30 minutes.
- Pour the broth and roast for 10 more minutes. Serve.

So, these are some interesting low-carb, adequate protein, and high-fat breakfast and lunch recipes. You can replace beef with mutton or chicken as per your taste.

Chapter 8- Keto dinner delicacies

It is time to prepare some delicious keto dinners. Please go through the following recipes for a healthy and yummy keto dinner.

1. Keto chicken veggie bowl

Net carbs: 3grams
Proteins: 14grams
Fats: 17grams
Calories: 193kcal
Serving size: 4
Ingredients:

- 1 tbsp butter
- 3 tbsp bacon fat
- 1 sliced onion and cabbage
- 2 minced garlic cloves
- Salt
- Pepper
- ½ tsp chili paste
- ¼ cup coconut aminos
- 4 shredded and cooked chicken breasts
- ½ tbsp sesame seeds

Preparation:

➢ Cook onions and garlic in oil and bacon fat.
➢ Add other ingredients and cook for 10 minutes till veggies become tender.
➢ Disperse some sesame seeds on the top. Serve.

2. Beef keto fajitas

Net carbs: 5grams
Proteins: 16grams
Fats: 22grams

Calories: 226kcal
Serving size: 4

Ingredients:

- 2 tbsp olive oil
- 1 cup cream
- 1 lb beef strips
- 1 green pepper and onion
- 2 garlic cloves
- 1 tsp paprika

- ½ tsp chili powder and garlic powder
- Salt
- Pepper
- ¼ cup lime juice

Preparation:

➢ Heat oil and add steak to it.
➢ Cook till it turns brown. Set aside.
➢ Fry onions and peppers and add cooked meat, spices, cream, lime juice, and garlic. Cook for 7 minutes and serve.

3. Cheesy mushrooms and meat

Net carbs: 1grams
Proteins: 6grams
Fats: 12grams

Calories: 178kcal
Serving size: 14

Ingredients:

- 4 meat slices
- 1 garlic clove
- 40 oz cream
- 1 egg
- 2 tbsp coconut flour

- 1 cup mozzarella
- Salt
- Pepper
- 16 oz mushrooms

Preparation:

➢ Preheat oven to 350F.
➢ Fry meat till it turns brown.
➢ Cut into pieces and reserve the fat residue.
➢ Pour the residue, meat pieces, and all ingredients into a bowl and combine.
➢ Place the mixture in a baking dish and drizzle butter.
➢ Bake till golden brown and serve.

4. Baked lamb chops

Net carbs: 1grams
Proteins: 20.8grams
Fats: 37.2grams
Calories: 423kcal
Serving size: 4

Ingredients:

- ½ cup grated Parmesan cheese
- 1 tsp garlic powder
- 1 tbsp parsley and avocado oil
- 1 tsp thyme, paprika, salt, pepper, and onion powder
- ¼ tsp chili powder
- 1/8 tsp oregano
- 4 lamb chops

Preparation:

- ➢ Preheat oven to 350F.
- ➢ Combine cheese and spices in a dish and coat the chops with it.
- ➢ Heat oil and fry the chops till they turn brown.
- ➢ Bake for 50 minutes. Serve.

5. Broiled salmon

Net carbs: 2.3grams
Proteins: 12grams
Fats: 16grams
Calories: 143kcal
Serving size: 4

Ingredients:

- 4 oz salmon fillets
- 1 tbsp mustard
- 2 minced garlic cloves
- 1 tbsp minced shallots
- 2 tsp mixed herbs
- ½ lemon
- Salt
- Pepper
- Lemon slices

Preparation:

- ➢ Combine all the ingredients in a bowl and spread generously over the salmon fillets.
- ➢ Broil for 8 minutes.
- ➢ Scatter some herbs at the top and serve with a lemon slice.

6. Creamy Tuscan chicken

Net carbs: 3.5grams
Proteins: 10grams
Fats: 21grams
Calories: 210kcal
Serving size: 4

Ingredients:

- 1 tbsp olive oil
- 4 chicken breasts
- Salt
- Pepper
- 1 tsp oregano
- 3 tbsp butter
- 3 garlic cloves
- 2 cups spinach
- ½ cup heavy cream

Preparation:

- ➢ Heat oil and cook the chicken breasts till brown. Set aside.
- ➢ Melt butter and add garlic, salt, pepper, oregano, and spinach. Cook till done. Add the cream and chicken and cook till sauce thickens. Serve.

7. Garlic shrimp zucchini pasta

Net carbs: 5grams
Proteins: 21.6grams
Fats: 34.3grams
Calories: 314kcal
Serving size: 3

Ingredients:

- 3 tbsp butter
- 1 lb peeled shrimp
- Salt
- Pepper
- 3 minced garlic cloves
- ¾ cup heavy cream
- ½ cup grated Parmesan cheese
- 1 cup cherry tomatoes
- 3 tbsp spiralized zucchini

Preparation:

- ➢ Melt some butter and fry shrimp. Set aside.
- ➢ Melt remaining butter and add garlic, Parmesan, tomatoes, salt, pepper, and cream to it.
- ➢ Cook for 10 minutes. Add the fried shrimp and zucchini.
- ➢ Combine and serve.

8. Instant pot butter chicken

Net carbs: 3grams
Proteins: 19grams
Fats: 29grams
Calories: 339kcal
Serving size: 8

Ingredients:

- 2 tbsp coconut oil
- 1 chopped onion
- 1 tbsp ginger-garlic paste
- 1 bowl chicken pieces
- 1 tbsp mixed spices
- Salt
- Pepper
- 1 cup unsweetened tomato sauce
- ½ cup fat-full coconut milk

Preparation:

- ➤ Rub the spice mix on the chicken. Set aside.
- ➤ Cook the onions, garlic, and ginger in the instant pot.
- ➤ Add chicken and cook till it turns brown.
- ➤ Stir the tomato sauce and coconut milk. Cook for 10 minutes. Serve.

9. Mutton butter bites

Net carbs: 6grams
Proteins: 36grams
Fats: 53grams
Calories: 644kcal
Serving size: 2

Ingredients:

- 1 bowl mutton pieces
- 1 cup butter
- 1 cup chopped onion and mixed vegetables
- 1 tsp garlic paste
- 1 tbsp mixed spices
- 1 cup bone broth
- 1 cup heavy cream

Preparation:

- ➤ In a large pot fry the meat, onion, and garlic paste in 2 tbsp butter for 3 minutes till it turns brown. Add the veggies, spices, and bone broth and boil.
- ➤ Add the cream and remaining butter and stir well.
- ➤ Cook for 10 minutes and serve.

Try these mouth-watering recipes for a perfect keto dinner. To know more recipes, keep reading further.

10. Instant pot keto beef stew

Net carbs: 7.8grams
Proteins: 34.3grams
Fats: 35.7grams
Calories: 514kcal
Serving size: 8
Ingredients:

- 1 chopped onion
- 2minced garlic cloves
- 2.65 lb boneless beef
- 4 chopped celery stalks
- Salt
- Pepper
- 1 tbsp paprika
- ½ tsp mixed spices
- 400grams tomatoes
- ½ cup bone broth
- 8 egg yolks

Preparation:

- ➤ Cut the beef into pieces. Set aside.
- ➤ Cook beef pieces, onion and garlic in the instant pot for 3 minutes.
- ➤ Add the tomatoes, paprika, spices, and celery.
- ➤ Cook for 20 minutes on high-pressure.
- ➤ Take out the extra liquid in a pan.
- ➤ Whisk the egg yolks with ½ cup bone broth.
- ➤ Combine the liquid and the egg yolk mixture and cook on low flame till the sauce is reduced.
- ➤ Mix the cooked beef with the sauce. Serve.

Chapter 9- Crunchy keto snacks

In this chapter, I will present some interesting keto snack recipes that you will love to munch.

1. Blackberry nut fat bombs

Net carbs: 1grams
Proteins: 4grams
Fats: 50grams
Calories: 392kcal
Serving size: 16

Ingredients:

- 2 oz crushed nuts
- 4 oz cream cheese
- 1 cup blackberries, coconut oil, and coconut butter
- 3 tbsp ricotta cheese
- ½ tsp vanilla essence and lime juice
- 3 drops Stevia

Preparation:

- ➢ Press the crushed nuts at the bottom of a mold.
- ➢ Bake for 5 minutes.
- ➢ Layer the baked nuts with cream cheese.
- ➢ Combine rest of the ingredients in a bowl in a smooth batter.
- ➢ Pour the batter over the cream cheese layer and freeze for 30 minutes. Serve.

2. Cheesy-meatball bites

Net carbs: 2grams
Proteins: 26grams
Fats: 28grams
Calories: 444kcal
Serving size: 3

Ingredients:

- 500grams minced beef
- 100grams cubed cheese
- 3 tbsp Parmesan cheese
- 1 tsp garlic powder
- Salt
- Pepper

Preparation:

- ➢ Combine salt, pepper, garlic powder, and beef.
- ➢ Enfold the cheese cubes in the mince and fry the meatballs. Serve.

3. Coconut boosters

Net carbs: 2grams
Proteins: 12grams
Fats: 16grams
Calories: 121kcal
Serving size: 6

Ingredients:

- 1 cup coconut oil
- ½ cup chia seeds
- 1 tsp vanilla extract
- 3 drops Stevia
- ¼ cup coconut flour

Preparation:

- ➢ Combine all the ingredients thoroughly in a bowl.
- ➢ Scoop out the mixture into muffin cups and freeze for 1 hour.
- ➢ Top with coconut flakes and serve.

4. Goat cheese artichoke dip

Net carbs: 3.2grams
Proteins: 7grams
Fats: 19grams
Calories: 116kcal
Serving size: 4

Ingredients:

- 14-ounce artichoke hearts can
- 1 pound goat cheese
- 2 tbsp olive oil
- 2 tsp lime juice
- 1 minced garlic clove
- 1 cup grated pecorino
- 1 tbsp mixed herbs
- Salt
- Pepper

Preparation:

➤ Pulse all the ingredients except pecorino in a food processor into a creamy paste. Sprinkle pecorino on the top and serve.

5. Keto Pretzels

Net carbs: 3grams
Proteins: 11grams
Fats: 18grams

Calories: 217kcal
Serving size: 2

Ingredients:

- 3 cups shredded mozzarella
- 4 tbsp cream cheese
- 1 ½ cups almond flour
- 2 tsp xanthan gum, yeast, warm water, and molten butter
- 2 eggs
- 1 tsp pretzel salt

Preparation:

➤ Preheat oven to 390F. Melt the mozzarella and cream cheese.
➤ Mix the yeast with warm water.
➤ Combine the almond flour, xanthan gum, eggs, yeast mixture, cheese mixture, and butter in a mixer into fine dough.
➤ Make 12 balls from the dough and roll into a pretzel shape.
➤ Arrange on a cookie sheet and coat with butter.
➤ Sprinkle the pretzel salt and bake for 15 minutes. Serve.

6. Keto brownies

Net carbs: 1grams
Proteins: 4grams
Fats: 9.6grams
Calories: 149kcal
Serving size: 2

Ingredients:

- ½ cup coconut oil
- 2 eggs
- ½ cup cocoa powder
- 5 Stevia drops
- Pinch of salt
- Unsweetened vanilla

Preparation:

- ➤ Preheat oven to 350F. Combine all the ingredients into a thick batter.
- ➤ Pour it into a loaf pan and bake for 20 minutes. Let it cool and then serve.

7. Stuffed mushrooms

Net carbs: 2grams
Proteins: 9grams
Fats: 18grams
Calories: 210kcal
Serving size: 20

Ingredients:

- 1 tbsp molten coconut oil
- 20 mushroom caps
- 1 pack turkey bacon
- 1 chopped cauliflower
- ¼ cup grated cheese
- ½ tsp minced garlic
- Salt
- Pepper
- 2 tbsp butter
- ½ cup chives

Preparation:

- ➤ Coat mushrooms with oil and place them upside down on a baking sheet and bake. Divide the bacon on a baking sheet and bake it.
- ➤ Boil the cauliflower florets and pulse in a mixer with cheese, garlic, salt, and pepper into a smooth puree.
- ➤ Stuff the mushrooms with the puree and top with crumbled bacon and butter. Serve.

8. Cheese crackers

Net carbs: 5.2grams
Proteins: 18grams
Fats: 39grams
Calories: 364kcal
Serving size: 8
Ingredients:

- 2 cups Parmesan cheese
- 1 cup almond flour
- 2 oz cream cheese
- 1 egg
- Salt
- 1 tsp rosemary

Preparation:
- Combine molten cheese, cream cheese, egg, salt, rosemary and almond flour in a bowl thoroughly into a fine dough.
- Place the dough on a parchment paper and spread it using a rolling pin.
- Cut into squares using a pizza cutter.
- Bake the crackers for 6 minutes on both sides till crispy. Serve.

9. Keto no-bake cookies

Net carbs: 3grams
Proteins: 5grams
Fats: 16.1grams
Calories: 174kcal
Serving size: 9
Ingredients:

- 2 tbsp butter
- ½ cup peanut butter
- 1 cup shredded coconut
- 4 drops vanilla Stevia

Preparation:

- Melt butter and add peanut butter to it.
- Add Stevia and coconut. Stir well.
- Spread the mixture on a sheet pan and freeze for 15 minutes. Serve.

10. Pumpkin fudge

Net carbs: 4grams
Proteins: 3grams
Fats: 13grams
Calories: 71kcal
Serving size: 20

Ingredients:

- 1 cup pumpkin puree
- 1 tbsp butter and coconut oil
- ½ tsp Stevia
- 2 tbsp coconut flour
- 1 tsp vanilla extract and cinnamon
- ½ tsp ginger and nutmeg
- 1/8 tsp clove powder
- Sea salt

Preparation:

- Combine all the ingredients at low flame.
- Line parchment paper on small line containers.
- Flatten the mixture into the containers.
- Refrigerate for 3 hours and cut into small squares. Serve.

These snack recipes are not only tasty; they are rich in fats and almost carb-free. Give each of these a try.

Chapter 10- Keto soups and salad recipes

Here are a few amazing keto soups and salad recipes. Please have a look.

Keto-friendly soups

1. Lemon chicken soup

Net carbs: 4grams **Fats: 15grams** **Serving size: 8**
Proteins: 11grams **Calories: 286kcal**

Ingredients:

- 10 cups chicken stock
- 3 tbsp olive oil
- 8 minced garlic cloves
- 1 diced onion
- Zest of 1 lemon

- 2 chicken breasts
- 1/2 tsp red pepper
- 2 ounces crumbled feta
- 1/3 cup chopped chive

Preparation:

- ➢ Sauté onion and garlic in some oil for 5 minutes.
- ➢ Add chicken, salt, pepper, lemon zest, red pepper, and chicken stock to the pot and boil the contents. Cook on medium flame for 15 minutes.
- ➢ Shred the meat from the chicken breasts with a fork and add feta and chive.
- ➢ Transfer to a bowl and serve.

2. Creamy cauliflower soup

Net carbs: 1.3grams **Fats: 4grams** **Serving size: 1**
Proteins: 11grams **Calories: 133kcal**

Ingredients:

- ½ tbsp olive oil
- 2 minced garlic cloves
- 1 diced onion
- 1 bowl cauliflower florets

- 32 ounces vegetable broth
- Salt
- Grated Parmesan cheese

Preparation:

- ➢ Sauté onion and garlic in some oil and cook till soft.
- ➢ Add cauliflower florets and vegetable stock and boil till cauliflower becomes soft. Transfer the contents to a mixer and blend into a fine soup.
- ➢ Adjust salt and serve with Parmesan cheese topping.

3. Instant pot beef-tomato soup

Net carbs: 4.1grams
Proteins: 21grams
Fats: 36grams

Calories: 433kcal
Serving size: 6

Ingredients:

- 1 tsp olive oil, minced garlic, and oregano
- 1lb minced beef
- 1 chopped onion
- 1/2 lb trimmed green beans
- 1 bowl diced tomatoes and bone broth
- Salt
- Pepper
- 1 cup Parmesan cheese

Preparation:

➢ Sauté beef in some oil using the sauté mode of the instant pot.
➢ Cook till it turns brown.
➢ Add onion, garlic, thyme, salt, pepper, tomatoes, bone broth, and oregano and let the contents boil. Add the beans and cover the lid.
➢ Cook on low pressure for 30 minutes. Top with cheese and serve.

4. Lamb soup instant pot

Net carbs: 2.2grams
Proteins: 30grams
Fats: 37grams

Calories: 462kcal
Serving size: 15

Ingredients:

- ½ cup tallow and vinegar
- 3 minced garlic cloves
- 1 diced onion
- ¼ cup rosemary leaves
- 3 diced celery sticks
- Salt
- Pepper
- 1 cup tomato paste
- 4 cups beef stock
- 4 pounds lamb bones
- ½ pound sliced mushrooms

Preparation:

➢ Sauté tallow, garlic, onion, celery, and rosemary for 5 minutes in instant pot.
➢ Add salt, pepper, vinegar, beef stock, and tomato paste.
➢ Now add the lamb bones and boil.
➢ Cover the lid and cook on low pressure for 4 hours.
➢ Strip the meat chunks from the bones before discarding.
➢ Add mushrooms and reduce the liquid by boiling. Serve.

5. Keto seafood chowder

Net carbs: 7.3grams
Proteins: 36grams
Fats: 44grams
Calories: 411kcal
Serving size: 4

Ingredients:

- 1lb chopped white fish
- 12 peeled shrimp
- 1 cup crab meat
- 1 diced onion
- 2 minced garlic cloves
- 4 cooked and chopped bacon slices
- 1 chopped radish
- 2 cup chicken stock
- 1 ½ cup coconut milk
- 2 tbsp coconut oil
- Salt
- Pepper

Preparation:

➢ Cook shrimp in coconut oil till it turns pink. Set aside.
➢ Now cook garlic, onion, salt, pepper, and radish for 5 minutes.
➢ Add fish, crab meat, and chicken stock and boil for 3 minutes.
➢ Add the shrimp back and cook on low flame for 15 minutes.
➢ Stir in the coconut milk and serve with crumbled bacon topping.

Fresh and healthy keto salads

6. Kale and blueberry salad

Net carbs: 2grams
Proteins: 4grams
Fats: 16grams
Calories: 191kcal
Serving size: 2

Ingredients:

- 6oz chopped kale
- 10 blueberries
- 1 tbsp sliced almonds
- ¼ sliced red onion
- 1 tbsp parsley and lime juice
- 2 tbsp olive oil
- Salt
- Pepper

Preparation:

- Assemble all the ingredients in a large bowl and toss to combine.
- Divide among plates and serve.

7. Tamari marinated steak salad

Net carbs: 4grams
Proteins: 33grams
Fats: 37grams
Calories: 500kcal
Serving size: 2

Ingredients:

- 75grams green salad
- 6 halved grape tomatoes
- 4 sliced radishes
- 1 tbsp olive oil
- ½ tbsp lime juice
- Salt
- 250grams steak
- ¼cup mustard sauce
- 1 tbsp avocado oil

Preparation:

- Marinade the steak in mustard sauce.
- Toss the veggies, olive oil, lime juice, and salt in a bowl.
- Divide the salad between two plates. Cook the steak in avocado oil.
- Cut into slices and distribute on each salad plate. Serve.

8. Smoked salmon salad

Net carbs: 1.3grams
Proteins: 10grams
Fats: 17grams
Calories: 125kcal
Serving size: 2

Ingredients:

- 1 bowl smoked salmon
- ½ cup blueberries
- 5 oz green salad
- 2 tbsp olive oil
- 1 tbsp vinegar

Preparation:

- ➤ Assemble all the ingredients except salmon in a bowl and toss to combine.
- ➤ Divide equally into two plates and top with smoked salmon. Serve.

9. Quail egg salad

Net carbs: 1grams
Proteins: 12grams
Fats: 15grams
Calories: 118kcal
Serving size: 1

Ingredients:

- 15 quail eggs
- 1 bowl grape tomatoes and chopped butter lettuce
- 1 grated carrot
- 7 crumbled bacon slices
- 1 tbsp olive oil and vinegar
- Salt

Preparation:

- ➤ Boil the quail eggs for 4 minutes and then put in cold water.
- ➤ Peel off the shell. Set aside.
- ➤ Place rest of the ingredients in a bowl and toss to combine.
- ➤ Add the eggs and toss again. Serve.

10. Turkey Arugula salad

Net carbs: 6grams
Proteins: 15grams
Fats: 20grams
Calories: 260kcal
Serving size: 2

Ingredients:

- 100grams arugula leaves
- 115grams diced turkey meat
- 10 blueberries
- Salt
- Pepper
- 1 diced cucumber
- 2 tbsp olive oil
- 2 tsp lime juice

Preparation:

➤ Assemble all the ingredients in a bowl and toss to combine. Serve.

Go keto with these healthy soups and salads.

Chapter 11: Delicious keto desserts

After all the tasty meals, it is time for some mouth-watering dessert. Here are a few great keto dessert recipes.

1. Red velvet donuts

Net carbs: 0.27grams
Proteins: 1.54grams
Fats: 5.34grams
Calories: 58.35kcal
Serving size: 2
Ingredients:
For donuts:

- 3/4cup almond flour
- 1/4cup flaxseeds
- 1/4cup erythritol
- 1tsp vanilla and baking powder
- 2 eggs
- 3tbsp coconut oil
- 1/4cup coconut milk
- 1tbsp cocoa powder
- 20 drops of red food color
- Salt

For pink keto icing:

- 1/4cup powdered erythritol
- 1tbsp coconut oil
- 2tbsp heavy cream
- 5 drops red food color

Preparation:

➢ Preheat oven to 350F.
➢ Combine the dry ingredients of the donut.
➢ Combine the wet ingredients and blend the two into a thick batter.
➢ Pour the batter into a donut tray and bake for 15 minutes.
➢ Combine the icing ingredients well and pour over the baked donuts.
➢ Set in the fridge for the icing to harden and then serve.

2. Coconut raspberry cupcakes

Net carbs: 3grams
Proteins: 5grams
Fats: 19grams
Calories: 225kcal
Serving size: 16

Ingredients:

For cupcakes:

- 1cup coconut flour and almond flour
- 7 eggs
- 1/2cup butter
- 1tbsp baking powder
- 3tsp vanilla extract
- Salt
- 3/4cup erythritol
- 1/2tsp Stevia liquid

For frosting:

- 16oz cream cheese
- 28 raspberries
- 1cup butter
- 1tbsp vanilla extract
- 1/4cup erythritol
- 1/2tsp Stevia liquid

Preparation:

- ➢ Preheat oven to 350F.
- ➢ Mix the cupcake ingredients in a bowl.
- ➢ Spoon in muffin molds and bake for 30 minutes.
- ➢ Melt butter and mix the frosting ingredients into it.
- ➢ Pour over the cupcakes and serve.

3. Cherry pie bars

Net carbs: 3grams
Proteins: 3.7grams
Fats: 9.1grams
Calories: 168kcal
Serving size: 12

Ingredients:

For crust:

- ½ cup butter
- 1 cup Stevia
- Salt
- 2 eggs
- 1/2tsp vanilla and almond extract
- 1 1/2cup almond flour

For filling:

- 1 cup de-seeded cherries
- 1/4cup water
- 1/2cup Stevia
- 1tbsp xanthan gum
- 1/4tsp almond extract

For glaze:

- 1/2cup Stevia
- 1/2tsp vanilla extract
- 2tbsp water

Preparation:

- ➢ Preheat oven to 350F.
- ➢ Combine the crust ingredients in a large bowl and whisk very well into a fluffy batter.
- ➢ Assemble filling ingredients and mix very well.
- ➢ Spread the filling over half of the batter on a baking pan.
- ➢ Then put spoonfuls of the remaining batter over the filling.
- ➢ Bake for 35 minutes.
- ➢ Mix the glaze ingredients and drizzle them on the cherry bars.

4. Peanut butter balls

Net carbs: 3.3grams
Proteins: 7.2grams
Fats: 15.1grams

Calories: 180kcal
Serving size: 15

Ingredients:

- 1 cup peanut butter and almond flour
- ¼ cup powdered Stevia
- 3oz unsweetened baker's chocolate

Preparation:

- ➢ Combine butter, flour, and Stevia very well and freeze for 2 hours.
- ➢ Melt the chocolate and make small balls from the frozen mixture.
- ➢ Poke a toothpick into each ball and dip it in the molten chocolate.
- ➢ Set in the fridge for 30 minutes to harden and serve.

5. Keto chocolate soufflé

Net carbs: 3.4grams
Proteins: 11grams
Fats: 25grams

Calories: 320kcal
Serving size: 4

Ingredients:

- 1 tbsp butter
- 1/3 cup monk fruit
- 5oz dark unsweetened chocolate

- 3 egg yolks
- 6 egg whites
- 1 cup coconut whipping cream

Preparation:

- ➢ Preheat the oven to 375F. Grease a soufflé dish with butter.
- ➢ Melt the chocolate and add whisked yolks.
- ➢ Blend egg whites and whipping cream vigorously.
- ➢ Combine egg mixture with chocolate mixture evenly.
- ➢ Pour the batter into soufflé dishes and bake for 20 minutes. Serve.

Go completely keto with these delicious dessert recipes. You may look for more options on various keto recipe books or magazines.

Chapter 12: Keto-friendly drinks

Please try these marvelous keto-drinks. You will absolutely love them.

1. Pumpkin spice latte

Net carbs: 5grams
Proteins: 1grams
Fats: 23grams
Calories: 235kcal
Serving size: 1

Ingredients:

- 1tbsp butter
- 1shot espresso
- 2tbsp erythritol
- 2tbsp pumpkin puree and coconut cream
- 1/4tsp pumpkin pie spice
- 1/2tsp cinnamon
- Salt
- 1/2cup almond milk

Preparation:

- ➤ Melt butter and turn it light brown on low flame.
- ➤ Brew some espresso and combine it with erythritol.
- ➤ Mix it with butter, cream, and pumpkin pie spice.
- ➤ Blend the contents in a mixer and pour into a glass. Serve.

2. Keto Butter beet

Net carbs: 2grams
Proteins: 0grams
Fats: 20grams
Calories: 200kcal
Serving size: 1

Ingredients:

- 1 1/2cup diet cream soda
- 2tbsp sugar-free butterscotch syrup
- 1/4cup heavy cream
- 1tsp vanilla essence
- 1tbsp erythritol powder

Preparation:

- ➤ Combine the butterscotch syrup with cream soda.
- ➤ Blend the heavy cream, erythritol powder, and vanilla in a bowl using a hand-mixer.
- ➤ Pour the mixture over the creamy-butterscotch syrup and serve.

3. Keto ice-tea

Net carbs: 1grams
Proteins: 1grams
Fats: 20grams
Calories: 200kcal
Serving size: 1

Ingredients:

- 1bag Thai tea
- 1/2cup boiling water
- Few ice cubes
- 1/4cup heavy cream
- 8 drops Stevia

Preparation:

- ➢ Place the tea bag in boiling water for 5 minutes.
- ➢ Pour the flavored water in a glass and drop few ice cubes in it.
- ➢ Add drops of Stevia and top with heavy cream.
- ➢ Stir well and serve.

4. Fat-burning vanilla smoothie

Net carbs: 4grams
Proteins: 12grams
Fats: 64grams
Calories: 650kcal
Serving size: 1

Ingredients:

- Yolks of 2 eggs
- 1/2cup mascarpone cheese
- 1/4cup water
- Ice cubes
- 1tbsp coconut oil
- 1/2tsp vanilla essence
- 1tbsp erythritol powder
- 1tbsp heavy cream

Preparation:

- ➢ Combine all the ingredients except cream in a mixer and pulse into a thick smoothie.
- ➢ Spoon out in a bowl, top with heavy cream, and serve.

5. Keto turmeric milkshake

Net carbs: 6.4grams
Proteins: 11grams
Fats: 19grams
Calories: 351kcal
Serving size: 1

Ingredients:

- 375ml coconut milk
- 2tbsp coconut oil
- 3/4tsp turmeric powder
- 1/2tsp ginger powder
- 1/4tsp cinnamon and vanilla
- 3 drops Stevia liquid
- 1/8tsp Himalayan salt
- Ice cubes

Preparation:

➢ Blend all the ingredients at high power for 30 seconds to form a thick golden shake.
➢ Pour into a glass and serve with cinnamon and turmeric topping.

With this, I end the recipe section of this book. Go to your kitchen and try these recipes. No wonder you will have a delicious keto menu throughout the week.

Conclusion

Ketogenic Diet is one of the most recommended and successful ways to shed weight. It has come as an answer to many people out there who were struggling due to over-weight and fighting daily battles with their own self.

Many people have gained back their lost confidence and charisma by going keto. You can be next. Give ketosis a genuine try and the results will speak for themselves. Let me quickly take you back through the points I covered in this book.

- ✓ Ketosis is a state of body that is achieved by following a low-carb, moderate-protein, and high-fat diet.
- ✓ It allows your body to become a fat burning machine.
- ✓ You should properly monitor your macros and calculate the intake of each.
- ✓ Know more about keto flu and how to get over it.
- ✓ Exercise a lot. It will help to make most from the ketosis.
- ✓ Formulate a diet chart for yourself.
- ✓ Make due preparations before going keto. It will ease many difficulties that you may encounter.
- ✓ Keep you keto staples and pantry ready.
- ✓ Process the veggies, freeze berries, make broths, and condiments. Be keto ready.
- ✓ Know what you should eat and drink in abundance and what you should avoid.
- ✓ Treat yourself every day with the marvelous keto recipes. Give each a try.

Dear readers, it is high time that you move out of your comfortable carb zone and step into the world of ketones. I am sure that you will see the wonderful results coming in no time. After all, who doesn't want to fit back into those completely forgotten skinny and slim-fit dresses?

All the best for you keto diet journey.

I hope you rediscover a more slim, fit, and confident version of yourself in just a few weeks. Keep calm and keto on!

Appendix I: Measurement Conversion Chart

Measurement mentioned	In grams	In ml	In Ounce
1 tbsp(tablespoon)	14.3 grams	14.78 ml	0.5 ounce
1 tsp(teaspoon)	4.2 grams	4.92 ml	0.16 ounce
1 cup	340 grams	236.5 ml	12 ounces
1 bowl (medium)	400 grams	450 ml	20 ounces
1 ounce	28.34grams	29.57ml	-
1 scoop(medium)	29grams	473.18ml	32fluid ounces
1 pound/lbs/lb	453.5grams	473.17ml	16ounces

Appendix II: Recommended Websites and books

https://ketodietapp.com/Blog/lchf/How-Many-Carbs-per-Day-on-Low-Carb-Ketogenic-Diet
https://www.perfectketo.com/keto-diet-tips/
https://www.ketovale.com/keto-flu/
https://www.healthline.com/nutrition/7-tips-to-get-into-ketosis#section7
https://ketodietapp.com/Blog/lchf/how-to-low-carb-15-common-weight-loss-mistakes
https://www.ketovangelist.com/keto-dos-and-donts/
https://www.perfectketo.com/how-to-exercise-in-ketosis/
https://ketodietapp.com/Blog/lchf/Ketogenic-Diet-FAQ-All-You-Need-to-Know#how_much_weight
https://www.perfectketo.com/keto-meal-prep/#2
https://www.womenshealthmag.com/weight-loss/g20135428/keto-dinner-recipes/?slide=12
https://ketosummit.com/ketogenic-diet-food-list#list
https://www.ruled.me/25-keto-dessert-recipes-valentines-day/
https://draxe.com/hub/keto-diet/keto-snacks/

Keto living day by day-a book by Kristie H. Sullivan
Quick Keto meals in 30 minutes-a book by Martina Slajerova
Keto: The Complete Guide to Success on The Ketogenic Diet, including Simplified Science and No-cook Meal Plans- a book by Maria Emmerich

CPSIA information can be obtained
at www.ICGtesting.com
Printed in the USA
LVHW100212211118
597873LV00004B/170/P